Bridget's Gambit

Women and the American West series

Bridget's Gambit

A Saga of Family Enterprise in Gold Rush California

Craig S. Harwood

University of Oklahoma Press : Norman

This book is published with the generous assistance of the McCasland Foundation, Duncan, Oklahoma.

Bridget's Gambit: A Saga of Family Enterprise in Gold Rush California is Volume 4 in the Women and the American West series

LCCN #2025034140
ISBN 978-0-8061-9655-8 (hardcover)

The manufacturer's authorized representative in the EU for product safety is Mare Nostrum Group B.V., Mauritskade 21D, 1091 GC Amsterdam, The Netherlands, email: gpsr@mare-nostrum.co.uk.

To Dyane, Avonlea, and Marilla

Contents

Preface

Although centered on the family matriarch, Bridget Miranda Shannon Evoy, this biography is as much about the triumvirate she formed with her daughters, Margaret Evoy McCourtney and Ellen Evoy Montgomery, to become a potent entrepreneurial force in California in the period of the Gold Rush and its emergence as a state. These working-class women overcame terrific adversity in their persistent quest to rise from poverty in Ireland and carve out a future in the American West. As a great-great-great grandson of Bridget I grew up hearing anecdotes about her and the larger family saga passed down through oral family tradition.

I was fascinated with the colorful personalities and dramatic events that inhabited these stories. Adding to the intrigue was the fact that the Evoy/McCourtney/Montgomery storyline so often intertwined with historically significant events and influential movers and shakers in California's early state history. Although aspects of her story have received some attention in the literature, it lacked the comprehensive treatment that it certainly deserved. Admittedly, Bridget was a difficult person to write about as primary source information on her life is rare. She was not interviewed during her lifetime and left no surviving diaries or journals. So much of what is known about her comes through the statements of her daughters, others acquainted with her, and public records. Additionally, as far as I was aware, no extant photographs of the matriarch survived. Hence, a detailed accounting of her life story, and indeed her very visage, remained obscure to me, as if she were a ghost on the periphery of my family history, tantalizingly out of reach. Then, through an unexpected stroke of luck, in 2024, another descendent, Carol Glover, was able to provide photographs of Bridget Evoy and Margaret McCourtney, finally putting faces to these compelling characters.

In the early phases of my career as a geologist, my travels within the Basin and Range Province of Nevada and the northern Sierras occasionally crossed through segments of the California Trail and Lassen's Cutoff that Bridget and her family had traversed. While hiking through the treeless canyons and furnace-like playas of the region, I frequently mused on the fragility of life in this stark and unforgiving setting. My thoughts often turned to an image of the fifty-nine-year-old Bridget riding on horseback at the front of the family wagon train on the punishing desert crossing, undaunted by the many threats to life and limb. I considered the unlikely survival of the family through the Sierran crossing, and I wondered how they persevered through this western landscape, equally hellish and majestic in its unspoiled, natural beauty. I found the story of the Irish matriarch and her daughters' journeys naturally compelling and one that seemed destined to be shared by some patient writer willing to engage in the relentless detective work needed to draw this story out of obscurity. Unexpectedly, but happily, that task fell on me. Inspired, I commenced exhaustive research, and in 2002, assembled an all-too-brief and therefore inadequate treatment of this compelling story. At that time, I set the manuscript aside in favor of another book project, which was ultimately published as *Quest for Flight: John J. Montgomery and the Dawn of Aviation in the West.* But over the succeeding years the fascinating story of the Evoy women continued to beckon like a voice searching for a vessel. In 2021 I decided to take on a full-length biography. On yearly family vacations to the Sierras, I returned again and again to the task of crafting the story, which I found flowed from my fingertips quite naturally in that inspiring setting. Much of the writing of this book, in fact, was carried out while making yearly pilgrimages to the Sierras.

Writing of events and characters from nineteenth-century America presents a challenge for a contemporary author, even one engaged in a biography focused on one family. Nineteenth-century societal attitudes as expressed in the period literature and even in personal correspondence are in many ways quite foreign to our modern sensibilities. Some terminology and attitudes expressed in the original sources can appear insensitive, offensive, and at times jarring to the modern researcher or reader. The story of the Gold Rush presents a particular conundrum for an author.

The process of western expansion and the California Gold Rush was profoundly consequential for the Indigenous peoples of California. Discrimination, exposure to disease, displacement, and governmental support of genocidal campaigns were all part of their stories. Despite this legacy, many tribal communities have remained resilient in the face of historic mistreatment and marginalization, showing great tenacity in persevering as distinct cultural entities, celebrating their cultural heritage, and preserving their customs, traditions, and languages. Since the close of the nineteenth century, many tribal communities have made significant progress in achieving federal recognition, financial compensation and aid, and reparations of certain ancestral tribal lands.[1] In recent decades, Indigenous organizations have taken the lead in launching environmental initiatives to restore inland waterways and gain federal protection of coastal marine preserves on the California coast in keeping with Indigenous tenets of land stewardship. These developments are testament to the strength and perseverance of Native peoples in California and nationally. I encourage readers wishing to explore the impact of nineteenth-century western expansion on Native Americans and Indigenous Californians to review the bibliography for further reading.

This biography focuses on the lives of one family across decades and regions. As much as possible, I have attempted to recount that story in a direct and unbiased manner without editorializing on the many larger, controversial aspects of western settlement and the Gold Rush. Others are writing those important stories. I hope that this book will be as enjoyable for you to read as it was for me to research, contemplate, and write.

Acknowledgments

My extensive research for this book required accessing numerous university libraries, historical societies, archival collections, and a few personal family history collections. Throughout this effort, I benefited from the generous assistance of many librarians, too numerous to name. For the researcher and author engaged in the pursuit of a literary project, our library professionals are our unheralded heroes! In my research I received invaluable assistance from the staffs of several historical societies, including the Nevada County Historical Society, Yuba County Historical Society, Shasta County Historical Society, Missouri Historical Society, Oakland History Center (Oakland Public Library), Trails West, Inc., Oregon–California Trails Association, Oakland History Museum, and the California Historical Society. The John J. Montgomery Collection at the Santa Clara University Archives and Special Collections contained important primary and secondary source material. I would like to acknowledge the encouragement of Nancy Leek of the Association for Northern California Historical Research, Robert Montgomery, Gary F. Kurutz, Gary Fogel, and the late Dottie Smith.[1] Mrs. Carol Glover was particularly generous in sharing her impressive family history research material and, importantly, for providing the only known surviving photograph of the main character of the story.

I thank several people at the University of Oklahoma Press for their help in transitioning the manuscript into a book. This project has benefited substantially from the guidance and input of Senior Acquisitions Editor Alessandra J. Tamulevich, who helped navigate the manuscript through the consideration and publication process. Important input and support came from Professor Renee M. Laegreid, who saw the potential of this story and championed its inclusion in OUP's Women and the American West series. I would like to thank Editorial Director Andrew Berzanskis for his willingness to take on this project, as well as his encouragement throughout. During the manuscript vetting process I received invaluable input and suggestions from Dee Garceau-Hagan (professor emerita of history, Rhodes College), Rose Marie Beebe (professor emerita of Spanish literature at Santa Clara University), and Robert M. Senkewicz (professor emeritus of history at Santa Clara University). I would like to thank Alice Stanton for guiding the manuscript through the copyediting phase, and Kirsteen Anderson for her excellent copyediting. These collective efforts provided the impetus and support that made this project possible. Finally, I am grateful for the support and input of Dyane Harwood, Avonlea Harwood, and Marilla Harwood, who reviewed and commented on portions of the manuscript.

Introduction

This biography follows the life of a family matriarch, Bridget Miranda Shannon Evoy, but also the saga an immigrant family, as they carved out a life of survival and eventually prosperity in the tumultuous trans-Mississippi West. Their saga intertwines with pivotal developments in nineteenth-century history, from transatlantic immigration to US westward expansion, frontier life in the Mississippi River port of St. Louis, the California Gold Rush, the formative years of California statehood, and the emergence of the San Francisco Bay Area as a major population center. Bridget Evoy came of age in rural Ireland in the closing decade of the eighteenth century, a time of great tumult in Europe. The American Revolutionary War, the decades-long French Revolution, and the 1798 Irish Rebellion all contributed to societal and political instability across the larger region. In Ireland, religious oppression and the initial phase of a devastating famine that began in the 1810s formed the backdrop of Bridget's formative years and early adulthood. Drawn by the promise of opportunity in America, Bridget and her young family made the transatlantic crossing, hoping to leave their hardships behind. Not long after their arrival on the American frontier in the burgeoning Gateway to the West, St. Louis, Missouri, Bridget's husband died, leaving her widowed with five children to support. She might have thought fate had snatched the American dream from her grasp, and in some respects it had. Reeling from personal tragedy, this widow and mother tapped a deep well of inner strength and persevered. Independent and driven, Bridget managed to eke out a modest livelihood as a farmer on the Missouri frontier. While the vulnerable young family struggled for survival, the American dream remained out of reach.

After a period of mourning, Bridget began a determined journey to overcome the hand that fate had dealt her. While economic growth in St. Louis fluctuated along with the larger patterns of trading and population surges throughout the 1830s and 1840s, the future for Bridget and her extended family remained insecure. Then, in mid-1848, news of the discovery of gold in the California Territory triggered the mass movement of hundreds of thousands of souls across the Great Plains to the then-distant and obscure California Territory. This "unsettling of the west" had major consequences for American society and culture and was the primary cause of the emergence of California on the larger economic landscape and its adoption as a US state. This westering migration was also, of course, profoundly devastating for Indigenous Americans throughout the trans-Mississippi West, a compelling topic for historians and Native American communities to this day, but one only tangential to this biography.

In the year of the forty-niners, Bridget and her adult sons and daughters saw the Gold Rush as a gambit for securing a more stable future. The family joined the mass emigration to this distant territorial outpost of the United States. None of the family members recorded their experiences on the Overland Trail at the time. However, contemporaneous journals, diaries, and post-trip letters from other emigrants traveling simultaneously with the Evoy/McCourtney clan shed some light on the family's westward journey. Those trail companions and acquaintances included well-known diarists such as J. Goldsborough Bruff, Hugh Heiskell, Rebecca Foster Reeve, and William Swain. After making the punishing journey across the plains and the Basin and Range Province of the inland West and barely surviving a harrowing winter crossing of the mountains of Northern California, Bridget and her family arrived in the goldfields with no more than they could carry on their backs. As the argonauts chased their gold-fever dreams and carved out a threadbare, hand-to-mouth existence around the mother lode, the family took a measured approach and began adroitly pulling the threads of opportunity in the California Territory. With the triumvirate of Bridget and her daughters Ellen Montgomery and Margaret McCourtney leading the way, this family launched diverse entrepreneurial enterprises that tapped into nearly every area of opportunity in the gold region. Recognizing where the group's strength lay, the male family members served in supporting roles of this potent, female driven family enterprise.

Doing business with prominent characters whose names would eventually grace the pages of history books, Bridget and her daughters pursued enterprises in merchandise and services, land deals, property management, moneylending, and transportation. Their property and business interests were inexorably tied to many emerging communities throughout Northern California, including Marysville, Yuba City, the Clear Creek mining district of the Shasta region, the Sierran gateway communities of Nevada City and Grass Valley, the Sacramento Delta region, the western addition of San Francisco, and eventually, the East Bay Area communities of Contra Costa and Oakland. Because of their strategic locations, these property holdings appreciated in value considerably during the 1850s and 1860s. As their entrepreneurship in the fledgling state lifted their position economically and socially, the family gained influence and used their hard-won strength to help those less fortunate. They dealt directly with some prominent shapers of the emerging state, including Tallman Rolfe, Pierson B. Reading, David Cheever, John A. Sutter, Major John Bidwell, William Myers, Peter J. Davis, and Stephen J. Field. They counted among their personal friends Joseph Le Conte, José Vicente Peralta, and Archbishop Joseph S. Alemany. Yet Bridget never forgot the adversity she had faced in her early life in rural Ireland, hardships that were inexorably linked with the economic situation, her religion, and prevailing societal attitudes toward the working class. In California, she and her daughters forged deep connections with the Catholic institutional hierarchy, fostering their influence and facilitating their charitable work supporting disadvantaged young women (such as orphans or those with disabilities).

One adversity Bridget, Margaret, and Ellen could not escape however was the fact of being female in a patriarchal society, one built upon the norms and attitudes of an era that marginalized women but also espoused a philosophy built upon profound contradictions. While a middle-class woman was assumed to be a pillar of moral strength and virtue, she was also considered to be delicate, dependent, and intimidated in the face of even mild adversity. Indeed, women were expected to be passive players within the economic landscape where men served as the power brokers. While expedient to the root ideals of patriarchy, these norms, emphasized in the schools and broadly promoted within the literature of the day, were unmoored from reality and, accordingly, were largely ignored on the frontier. Bridget, Ellen, and Margaret ignored prevailing attitudes, pushed through fronts of resistance, and generally transcended the bounds of patriarchy with apparent ease. In fact, the mid-nineteenth century saw the emergence of a feminist movement in California with activists such as Eliza Farnham, Georgia Bruce Kirby, and Clarina Howard Nichols leading the way in giving voice to women's issues. On a national level, luminaries like Mary Virginia Terhune, Charlotte Perkins Gilman, and Margaret Fuller were active in literary and intellectual circles as well. The "salt of the earth" Evoy women did not engage in these movements. As their activist sisters agitated public opinion in favor of suffrage and other rights due to women, Bridget, Margaret, and Ellen led by example in their own personal, yet very determined way. Their march up the ladder of social and economic status was as inexorable as the public campaigns of their activist sisters-in-arms, offering powerful role models of independence and assertiveness in the then-male-dominated fields of business and real property.

The publication of this compelling saga comes 177 years after the family arrived in the then-distant outpost of the western frontier, hoping against hope that their gambit for survival, renewal, and prosperity would, in the parlance of the forty-niners, "pan out." Their compelling story, heretofore lost to time, offers a tantalizing glimpse into the life experiences of a remarkable group of women. It is my privilege to share this fascinating saga.

CHAPTER 1

A New Beginning

The remnant of our people,
Sweeping westward, wild and woeful,
· Like the cloud-rack of a tempest,
Like the withered leaves of autumn

Lady Jane Wilde, 1887

The hills and dales of coastal Ireland are made lush through a gift of the Gulf Stream, a major oceanic current that flows offshore. This verdant growth blanketing the countryside of southeastern Ireland hints at the reason for Ireland's moniker—the Emerald Isle. It was here in the year 1791 when the extended Shannon family gathered in a thatched cottage on the lands of Rosegarland Estate, County Wexford to celebrate the birth of a daughter, Bridget Miranda Shannon. As tenants on the country estate, the Catholic Shannons, like the majority of the local population, descended from people who had engaged in agriculture for generations. Despite the bucolic setting and the land's agricultural potential, the economy of rural Ireland was strained, and survival for agrarian families required resourcefulness and terrific resilience.[1] For the Irish peasantry, life was inexorably tied to the cyclical pattern of tilling, sowing, and harvesting. Owned by a member of the gentry who served in the British Parliament, Robert Leigh (1729–1803), Rosegarland was a 650-acre estate encompassing a streamside terrace along the meandering Corock River. The Shannons rented acreage on the estate, where they raised animals and

6

maintained a plot where they grew vegetables such as the ubiquitous potato and perhaps oats and barley in some larger fields.
Hence, they were subject to the economic limitations of their
livelihood. Absentee landlords regarded their Irish landholdings as a source of income and viewed the countryside as a hostile place to live.[2] Thus, they ignored their peasant tenants unless
they fell behind in paying rent, in which case they were sooner or
later evicted from their homes, leading many to turn to survival
through the charity of an already impoverished community.

Irish society in the period was rural, hierarchical, and familial
in the sense that the family unit superseded the individual. The
family, or kin group, often comprised up to three or four generations. Details of Bridget Shannon's early years are obscure.
As was typical for children in rural Ireland, she participated in
the family economy from a very early age. On the farm, life and
work reflected societal norms of the period; the roles for children
within the family economy were typically segregated by gender and
age.[3] Young girls normally would work closely with their mothers,
and perhaps aunts and grandmothers, and would be expected to
help care for their younger siblings. Bridget served this role for
her younger sister, Margaret. The boys in the family usually would
work with the men outdoors helping with the more physical farm
labor, such as herding animals, cleaning corrals and animal pens,
repairing fences and irrigation, cultivating grainfield crops, and
digging turf (peat) for use as a building material or as fuel in
the home hearth. Working with the women in her home, Bridget
would have learned skills passed down through the generations:
cooking, sewing, spinning and weaving wool, and cooking.[4] Occasionally, she would be tasked with duties on the farm: collecting
eggs, drawing water from the well, grooming the horses, assisting
with shearing sheep, and other duties not fulfilled by the boys.
Girls' roles were well defined within the framework of a patriarchal society. They were encouraged to be obedient and to exhibit
self-control.[5] Bridget was expected to learn the skills necessary for
family life, and later as she reached her teens, how to manage a

household and rear children. Her formative years would prepare her for a role as a homemaker, wife and mother.

Unlike many working-class Irish women of her era, Bridget was literate. Her access to education was influenced by the family's religious affiliation and the seasonal patterns of farming. In keeping with religious biases of the time, under the existing penal laws, only children of the Anglican faith were allowed to attend public schools. No provision was made to finance schools for the Catholics who populated many areas of Ireland. Instead, Catholics and Presbyterians discreetly pursued education through small, informal "hedge schools," or *scoil chois claí*, which met in private homes and were technically illegal.[6] During the planting and harvest seasons, in which children played an integral part, Bridget and her siblings would need to be withdrawn from school. However, the convenience of home-schooling in scoil chois claí helped to minimize this disruptive pattern.

The Shannons maintained a small farm on a homestead within the expansive Rosegarland Estate. Many tenants like them lived in conditions that were not unlike those their ancestors had known since the Middle Ages and before.[7] A typical tenant home was a one-room hut of waddle-and-daub construction with a thatched roof supported by hewn timber beams. It typically had a compacted earthen floor and lacked windows. Some homes were made from stacked stones, either dry stacked or bonded with mud mortar, the outside covered in whitewash to seal the moisture out. Some shelters were constructed of stacked turf (peat). The only source of heat within these hovels was a stone-lined fireplace. To retain the heat, these structures lacked chimneys, so the smoke from the fire lingered above the heads of the occupants and dissipated through the thatched roof. These structures, if well maintained, could last for many decades and, accordingly, some were passed down through familial lines for several generations. The hearth was the focus of much daily activity, especially in the chilly winter months when family members would gather around the hearth and share local news, tell the children traditional folktales,

A typical cottage of the working-class Irish family, in which two or more generations would live.

and perhaps sing shanties or *sean nós* in the old style or engage in gossip. Furniture and cooking facilities were primitive, and the family's diet was mediocre, monotonous, and inadequate.

But events playing out on the larger European stage could come home to citizens, even to the inhabitants of rural Ireland. As the eighteenth century drew to a close, a spirit of discontent and intolerance emerged in Europe, heightening anxiety for rulers and their governments. This tumult was punctuated by revolutionary conflicts in France and the recent British defeat by its errant American colony. Ireland also echoed with rumblings of discontent and strife as the nation experienced myriad political, economic, and societal hardships. Consequently, working-class Irish families suffered immensely. This adversity had its roots in a population divided by religion and socioeconomic inequalities, exacerbated by the fact that a small percentage of the population enjoyed a disproportionate amount of power and wealth. As the peasantry struggled, the gentry remained concerned with the implications of political instability for their own fortunes. The atmosphere was ripe for rebellion. In the late spring of 1798, as Bridget reached her seventh year, the simmering discontent on the home front gave impetus to a major Irish uprising against the British Crown. Widespread sectarian violence erupted across southeast coastal Ireland, much of it centered in County Wexford. The main organizing Irish force was the Society of United Irishmen, an underground republican group of citizens inspired by the recent American and French revolutions. Although the leadership of the Wexford rebels consisted of both Catholics and Protestants, the rank and file were largely Catholic.[8] Several battles were fought within the coastal reaches of County Wexford, bringing the conflict into the Barony of West Shelmaliere and within earshot of the formerly quiescent hamlet of Rosegarland. As the combatants skirmished in the countryside, local residents waited anxiously for news of developments, and of casualties. It is likely that some of Bridget's extended family and neighbors became involved in the rebellion, whether through providing material and logistical support or engaging directly in the hostilities. Women assisted however they could; sharing intelligence on enemy movements, hiding weapons, or running safe houses.[9] Only in County Wexford did the United Irishmen rebel forces meet with notable success. In response to the government forces' killing of prisoners at New Ross, the rebels killed more than one hundred local loyalists at Scullabogue (five miles north of Rosegarland) and another hundred at Wexford Bridge.[10] These towns and hamlets comprised close-knit communities where everyone knew everyone, and Bridget's family would have been touched by the tragedy. The rebellion was ultimately crushed at the battle of Vinegar Hill, County Wexford, in the summer of 1798. As a consequence of the rebellion, a pall was cast over the immediate future of the Irish folk, already struggling to survive in an increasingly depressed economy. Unrest in the southern coastal counties would continue into the early 1820s.

As the Irish population grew in the first decades of the nineteenth century, the nation struggled to provide for its citizens, especially the working class. Opportunities for employment in manufacturing diminished and the great bulk of the population had to find a living in agriculture. The fragmentation of landholdings also impacted rural families. When a male family member got married, the father subdivided his land and assigned a portion of the acreage to the groom. As families were large and holdings generally small, this led to the division of land into increasingly smaller plots, too small for growing grain or corn or other row crops.[11] These small parcels could only sustain basic crops like the potato and, since potatoes could not be efficiently stored, the rural population was vulnerable to crop failure. Complete dependence on casual and seasonal labor became the reality for an increasing number of Ireland's rural population. This reality plus the constraints of land tenure was often a route by which Irish tenants were pushed further into poverty.[12] Humanitarians became increasingly concerned about the fate of the Irish poor while the politicians turned a blind eye to their plight.

Against this backdrop of political, religious and economic adversity in Ireland, Bridget Miranda Shannon came of age. In about the year of 1820, Bridget, began a courtship with James Evoy, a local man who also hailed from a Catholic family. Their respective families most likely knew one another and a union may have been encouraged or even arranged. After a brief courtship, the young couple married. In the era a woman was expected "to fulfill herself in the 'instinctive' arts of child rearing, domestic pursuits, and spiritual comfort."[13] It was thought that the foundational ideal of marriage kept society stable. As they began their new life, they most likely lived with either the Evoys or the Shannons. But as dark clouds gathered on the horizon, they pondered an uncertain future. As the new century dawned, a new adversity would soon emerge for the Irish citizenry. The British government's long-held policy supported large-scale reliance on a single agricultural product, the potato, whose vulnerability to crop disease suggested a disaster in waiting. The result was crop failure in 1817 and again in 1822 during which time the Irish peasantry suffered terribly from famine and disease.[14] These were merely the first pangs of the later Great Famine of the 1840s. These are the circumstances in which Bridget and James began their union and considered starting a family of their own. In the Victorian ethos, motherhood was valued as the most fulfilling and essential of all women's duties. They were expected to uphold moral and social standards while simultaneously tending to their family's needs. As she transitioned into young adulthood, Bridget appears to have worked within this traditional framework, but she would not do so for long. As events unfolded, some societal norms would have to yield. This young woman was cut from a different cloth.

Bridget and James may have been allocated a small plot of land (a portion of either the Evoy or the Shannon farms) to establish a subsistence crop and maintain livestock. Beginning in the early 1820s, they began a family with the birth of Mary Ann (1821), Margaret (1824), and John (1825). Throughout this period, the economic conditions worsened for rural Irish communities, and the Evoys' future appeared increasingly grim. Widespread crop failures in 1826 and 1827 led to the discussion of new emigration schemes that received considerable support.[15] Meanwhile, Irish and British politicians failed to address the dwindling resources for land and labor through domestic policies. Instead they promoted a self-serving solution—the idea of emigration. In essence, the fate of the Irish peasantry was in their own hands. Facing religious conflict, lack of political autonomy, and dire economic conditions in the British Isles, the Scotch-Irish immigrants were drawn to America by the promise of landownership and the prospect of greater religious freedom. The initial immigration of Irish in the late 1820s predated the much more widely known large-scale exodus during the Irish potato famine, or Great Hunger, of 1846–51. Unfortunately, this mass exodus from the Old Country didn't significantly improve the situation for those left behind. Irish poet Lady Jane Wilde lamented the loss of the Irish people: "Scarcely a million and a half are left of people too old to emigrate, amidst roofless cabins and ruined villages, who speak that language now. Exile, confiscation, or death, was the final fate written on the page of history for the much-enduring children of Ireland. . . . They fled across the Atlantic like a drift of autumn leaves—'pestilence-stricken multitudes.'"[16]

By the late 1820s, the Evoys evidently concluded that relocating to America could offer salvation from their otherwise grim prospects. In a common pattern, James would travel first to establish a toehold for the family in the United States and, once situated, would send for his family. Although Bridget was early in her pregnancy with her fourth child, sometime near the end of 1827, James made the transatlantic passage to America. In short order, James traveled to the Missouri frontier and settled on land in Hancock Prairie in Callaway County, some seventy-five miles west of the city of St. Louis. Despite the popular image of the American melting pot, the famine immigrants faced both anti-Irish and anti-Catholic prejudice in America. Much of the anti-Catholic bias focused on a fear of papal influence and authority. To many nativist Americans, the idea that Catholics professed allegiance to a foreign religious leader raised doubts about whether they could ever be "truly" American. St. Louis, however, provided a somewhat more tolerant environment for the Irish, especially since Irish Catholics shared a religious heritage with the French and Creole founders of the original village of St. Louis. Several religious organizations helped build communities within this frontier city, where a stronghold of Irish immigrants and Irish-themed charitable societies provided logistical support and limited financial assistance to immigrants making the transition from the Old Country to the western frontier of nineteenth-century America. In early 1828, James purchased 160 acres of property in Hancock Prairie.[17] This purchase may have been possible through a loan. As the initial weeks of 1828 passed, Bridget awaited word from James and prepared for the birth of their third daughter, Ellen Bridget Evoy.

In late April 1828, shortly after Ellen's birth, Bridget settled her affairs, said her goodbyes to her extended family and friends, and took the leap of faith into a new life. Her children ranged from a newborn up to the age of seven years. Their journey commenced with passage by ship to Liverpool, the main port of embarkation for transatlantic travel. Here the family boarded a steam packet ship for the Atlantic crossing.[18] The prospect of a long oceanic crossing may have seemed like a great adventure to her children, but it promised to be an ordeal for a single caregiver responsible for four children. Bridget would be tested. In that period the Atlantic crossing by packet sailing ship was an arduous undertaking that typically took between eighteen and twenty days for the fastest ships. Packet ships carried mail, cargo, and people, but most emigrants were confined to the steerage area belowdecks, referred to as the "tween decks." The steerage area was normally crowded, dark, and damp, infested with rats, insects, and disease. Limited sanitation and the effects of sea sickness often combined to make the confined space extremely unpleasant.[19] These passengers suffered greatly from poor weather and rough seas over the course of two-and-a-half to three weeks' travel. For Bridget, comforting and entertaining her toddlers, keeping the peace between the children, and caring for her newborn would have been an extremely taxing experience affording little sleep other than what came through sheer exhaustion.

The Evoys arrived in port at Baltimore, Maryland, sometime in the early summer of 1828, with James likely greeting the ship at the docks.[20] The reunion of the young family would have been joyous; however, the novelty of this unfamiliar and exotic land was secondary to the pressing need to make the long journey to the Missouri frontier and their Hancock Prairie homestead. Their journey took several weeks by wagon through remote terrain west of the Appalachians.

Sometime between mid-1829 and early 1830, Bridget gave birth to her last child, James. In 1830 the Evoys relocated to Bonhomme Township within St. Louis County. At the time St. Louis was a bustling but small river port city with a population of a little more than 5,800.[21] In 1830 James and Bridget sold property to William T. Christy, the scion of a prominent member of St. Louis society. Christy (1803–83), a major landowner, had been purchasing sizable sections of North St. Louis extending back to the time of the city's founding at the dawn of the century. A member of the "Irish crowd," Christy was a community leader who supported his fellow Irishmen through the Erin Benevolent Society. James was a competent public speaker and was tapped for these skills by a good friend who was running for political office. While on a political speaking tour in 1830, James contracted pneumonia. After several weeks his condition worsened and in August he died of complications.[22] Bridget was suddenly faced with a profound personal crisis. Devastated and alone in this frontier settlement, half a world away from home and without the support of relatives, she faced sole responsibility for the welfare of her children.

Given her circumstances and the prevailing attitudes of the day, Bridget faced precious few options outside of pursuing remarriage to a suitor who could provide financial security. This was an extension of the Victorian notion of women serving in a dependent or passive role. Defined as such, women were generally circumscribed socially and especially economically. Popular writings geared to a female audience implied a woman should serve as a pillar of moral strength and virtue but also portrayed her as delicate and prone to illness.[23] These attitudes and norms affirmed men's dominance in society, the very definition of a patriarchal system. Many women, however, especially those in straitened economic circumstances, failed to follow the norms to some degree or another. Bridget was one of these women.

While women could find jobs as shop girls or factory workers, female wage earners were considered unnatural. In addition, low wages, the absence of upward mobility, and depressing and unhealthy working conditions all made marriage an attractive survival strategy for working-class women.[24] As events will show, however, a fiercely independent and determined widow soon emerged. She began to shed the constraints of her era and embark on a journey of assertive womanhood. Her choices would often transgress the traditional options afforded to women. She drew strength from within.

The widow divided her time between rearing her children and overseeing a working farm at Hancock Prairie. As ranch boss, she directed the daily activities of laborers and perhaps her oldest son, John. Always the ardent equestrian, she occasionally rescued stray horses and, after posting advertisements to find their owners, adopted these animals for life on her ranch. Sometime after James Evoy's death, Bridget purchased a house in St. Louis adjacent to St. Louis University.[25]

Located at the confluence of the Missouri and Mississippi Rivers, St. Louis was at the strategic center of one of the two great inland water transportation systems of the continental United States.[26] Because the city stood at a point where the channel of the Upper Mississippi deepened, it became the terminus of nearly all boats and all cargo traveling up and down the river.[27] The city's residents capitalized on the role of the steamboat in the regional economic landscape. The city profited to a great extent from its proximity to the trailheads of the overland trails, located in the frontier towns of Independence, St. Joseph, or Westport, Missouri. All travelers on the Oregon Trail, the Mormon Trail, or the Santa Fe Trail passed through St. Louis, which was the outfitting location for practically all the overland journeys into the trans-Mississippi West.[28]

Although St. Louis stood out as a hub of commerce and transportation on the western US frontier, other segments of the local economy were less lucrative. Sustaining a living through agriculture in the Missouri frontier was difficult in the best of circumstances. As a single widow with several children, the odds were that the Evoy family would descend into the very type of poverty they had escaped in Ireland. But Bridget showed no inclination to remarry for financial stability or to rely on charity for survival. She focused her energies on managing the farm and its modest returns from the sale of grain. If she worked hard and persevered, she hoped she might maintain a viable revenue stream and elevate the family's status financially.[29]

Largely because of its role as the major gateway to the trans-Mississippi West, St. Louis grew considerably starting in about 1830 (population 6,252), with a marked increase after 1834 when a new pulse of emigration commenced. The city's growth continued steadily, and by 1840 the population reached 22,640, representing an increase of more than 250 percent.[30] Although many new arrivals in St. Louis were passing through on their way to the overland trails, those who did settle in the city increased the pressure for land, and property values increased, albeit at a modest pace. Perceiving an opportunity, Bridget began to venture into real estate to supplement her income. Her associations with Catholic and Irish organizations led to her making the acquaintance of influential St. Louis citizens. This network inevitably provided opportunities for the ambitious widow, who made numerous land deals with such

The bustling waterfront commercial district of St. Louis, the "Gateway to the West." *London Illustrated News*, 1858.

prominent St. Louis landholders as William Christy and Captain James W. Kingsbury. Small-scale real-estate investments involved purchasing, leasing, and selling land or extending mortgages to buyers, although returns were muted in this frontier marketplace. She occasionally entered into legal actions involving leases or mortgage lending contracts. Naturally, her self-reliance and determination to survive as an independent financial player placed her at odds with societal gender norms, but in a recurring theme throughout her life, she refused to be restricted in her choices.

Bridget's family had been associated with the Roman Catholic congregation of the Sisters of St. Joseph of Carondelet and, in keeping with her own upbringing, she made sure her daughters were educated within Catholic organizations. Due to the lack of public schools in the period, religious organizations initially provided education for all children within the city, Catholic and non-Catholic alike. The curriculum at these schools was limited to religious instruction and basic "book learning" that would enable a mother later to continue to educate her children at home. The Catholic missions provided housing for orphans, taught through their ministries, and in the case of the Sisters of St. Joseph, provided support and resources for deaf children through the St. Joseph Institute for the Deaf, which remains at the forefront of deaf education to this day. Interestingly, Bridget's granddaughter Margaret Montgomery would later take vows as a nun with the Sisters of St. Joseph of Carondelet convent in the early 1880s.[31] As her daughters matured and entered young adulthood, Bridget, Mary Ann, Margaret, and Ellen would become active in charitable activities with the Catholic missions. This work was typically focused on supporting and finding suitable homes for girls and young women who were orphaned, who were deaf or blind, or who came from otherwise difficult circumstances. In various ways, the Evoy women continued a tradition of charitable work for the remainder of their lives.

Bridget's independent disposition would have a strong influence on how her daughters would fit (or not fit) into the mold of womanhood as conceptualized in the era. This and the fact that she was the sole parent established her as a strong female role model for her daughters, who would not know a father figure except for perhaps a priest from their congregation. This legacy of independence would play out in various ways. While in more formal social settings they donned Victorian fashion (bustle dresses or ball gowns), in their daily lives they opted for practical clothing suited to farm life. The salt-of-the-earth pragmatism required to maintain a farm was unavoidable. Like other frontier women, they rolled up their sleeves and engaged in the physical work of caring for animals, planting and harvesting, collecting the animal products (eggs, milk), and carrying out the myriad duties required to eke an existence from the land.[32] They embraced their independence. At the age of twenty, Bridget's eldest daughter, Mary Ann Evoy, requested her own listing in the city directory, a symbolic statement of independence as a single woman coming of age in the community. At the age of twenty-two, in 1846, Margaret Evoy married a St. Louis man in his late twenties named John Hamilton McCourtney, who made his living as a blacksmith, marine mechanic, and engine builder.[33] The following year, Mary Ann married a local man named Joseph D. Mullikin, a ship's carpenter.[34] Both McCourtney and Mullikin worked in trades that served the local riverine port economy driven by the steamboat shipping industry.[35] The Evoy, Mullikin, and McCourtney families may well have belonged to the same Catholic parish and participated in the same organizations, so would have been acquainted with one another socially. They had in common the shared the experience of being subjected to anti-Irish and anti-Catholic sentiment of the era. Mullikin and McCourtney were nearly three decades junior to the forceful family matriarch and, perhaps not surprisingly, they soon recognized the hierarchy within the family and hence deferred to Bridget.

In the opening months of 1848, events were playing out in the distant California Territory that, although not fully understood initially, would ultimately have widespread repercussions for the nation. Rumors and claims of gold strikes in the Sierra Nevada range began to circulate in the press, stimulating much public discussion and speculation. In response, California's military governor, Colonel Richard B. Mason, personally visited the gold-fields to verify the tales of gold strikes along the American River.[36] Mason's report of that trip prompted President James Polk to make an official announcement of the gold discovery in his State of the Union address to Congress on December 5, 1848. Many historians view this official confirmation as a crucial impetus of the California Gold Rush. The chance discovery of mineral wealth and its alleged ubiquity across the Sierran landscape thrust the backwater territory onto the world stage, triggering an epochal emigration to this remote American territory. People carving out a meager livelihood on the periphery of the trans-Mississippi West endured a toilsome life. For many of those people, the notion of harvesting gold from the streams of California appeared an easy get-rich-quick scheme that, if they were lucky, would uplift their station in life. The allure of alleged easy wealth tempted a broad cross section of society. Of this phenomenon Gold Rush historian JoAnn Levy has noted: "No expression characterized the Califor-nia gold rush more than the words 'seeing the elephant.' . . . For gold rushers, the elephant symbolized both the high cost of their endeavor—the myriad possibilities for misfortune on the journey or in California—and like the farmer's circus elephant, an exotic sight, an unequaled experience, the adventure of a lifetime."[37]

Their interest piqued, Bridget and her family found the chi-mera of prosperity in the far West too tempting to resist. The family matriarch made the case, apparently convincingly, that the family should relocate to the California Territory. Although they couldn't know it at the time, this leap-of-faith decision would require each family member to draw on their reserves of tenacity and mental toughness. Regardless, with the family decision made, the die was cast.

CHAPTER 2

Leap of Faith

He who rides the back of the tiger cannot dismount at will.

Chinese adage

The plan to uproot the extended family and embark on a momentous westering journey evoked themes of renewal and of hope, familiar themes for Bridget. Her proposal of venturing through the vast expanse of western territory was as bold as it was risky. Over the winter of 1848–49, Bridget, Margaret, and Margaret's husband, John McCourtney, collectively liquidated their real properties and other assets and prepared for the next phase of their lives. They were committed to carving out a future in the California Territory: The journey would be a one-way trip. Bridget's daughter Mary Ann Mullikin elected to stay in St. Louis with her husband but would eventually relocate to California several years later.

As the news of the California gold discovery played out in the media, the unprecedented public reaction had important consequences for the American nation. If one believed the rumors circulating publicly, wealth in the mountains of California was within reach of the everyman. The majority of forty-niners were ignorant of the exigencies and risks involved in the overland journey. Americans considered the territory west of the 100th meridian to be a vast and desolate expanse of land, which geographers referred to as the Great American Desert, a broad region that encompassed the Great Plains, the Continental Divide region and the

Great Basin to the west.[1] The few maps published in guidebooks of the late 1840s were typically not vetted and some were based in large part on speculation and hearsay. Some of the more popular guidebooks of the day included Joseph Colton's *Western Tourist and Emigrant Guide* (1846), John C. Frémont's *Report of the Exploring Expedition to the Rocky Mountains in the Year 1842, and to Oregon and North California in the Years 1843–1844* (1845), Lansford Hasting's *The Emigrant Guide to Oregon and California* (1845), and Edwin Bryant's *What I Saw in California* (1848). Of the available sources, Joseph Ware's *Emigrant's Guide to California* (1849) enjoyed great popularity with emigrants.[2] Many who gathered and prepared for their journey at the "jumping-off" settlements of Independence and St. Joseph, Missouri, were respectable, law-abiding individuals. But among the swelling masses of argonauts were marginal characters seeking to escape from some adversity brought on by their own deeds or in some cases, forces beyond their control. One diarist, an attorney, commented that the multitude of "hard cases" he saw on the streets of Independence were "armed to the teeth."[3] But these problematic characters were a minority within the emigration. Tens of thousands of average folks upended their lives and took a leap of faith during this transformative event in American history.

The encampments at the trailheads were awash with frenetic activity, many people chomping at the bit to begin their momentous adventure. But no amount of ambition could suppress the realities presented by mother nature. As a practical matter, the journey to the California Territory was bookended by the seasonal weather patterns. The onset of late spring at the Missouri frontier marked the commencement of westering at one end, and the onset of winter in the Sierra Nevada served as the other end of overland travel. Emigrants who gathered and outfitted their groups at the jumping-off points in Missouri in the late spring of 1849 had to wait for two crucial elements before beginning their journey westward: (1) the ebbing of the spring runoff so that the large rivers and streams could be forded by wagon trains, and

(2) the commencing of spring growth of wild grasses for livestock foraging en route. The livestock powered the transportation and the grasses provided the fuel. The pace of travel maintained by the emigrants between the Missouri and Sierra Nevada endpoints dictated their fate: Laggards ran the risk of being pinned down in the mountains by winter storms. This point cannot be overemphasized. The emigrants embarking from the trailhead would have to wage an unrelenting battle against adversity. Attrition would take a daily toll.

After acquiring livestock (horses, oxen, and mules), food, a few wagons, personal supplies, and the tack necessary for overland travel in early May 1849, Bridget and family traveled to the trailhead at Independence, Missouri, set up base camp, and prepared for the months-long overland journey. While biding their time at camp, they took on the important work of preparing the wagons, stocking the train's larder, and training the teams of oxen to work in pairs in the yoke. Bridget's experience with livestock and horses undoubtedly proved useful in the training and care of the animals. The Evoy women would have supplied the company's field kitchen with foodstuffs that could last for a few months or longer: canned fruit and vegetables; dried, salted, or smoked beef; and cooked and preserved food that maintained a shelf life and could serve as a backup when cooking over an open fire was impossible.

The time waiting at the trailhead also provided opportunities for the Evoy and McCourtney families to become acquainted with other travelers who might choose to join forces with them and form a larger wagon train. These initial interactions with fellow travelers would inevitably give rise to an informal pecking order within the train. Newcomers joining the Evoy/McCourtney train would soon realize Bridget's assertiveness. Her maturity and experience operating a farm as ranch boss prepared her to serve as a clear-headed, calming influence, someone who could participate in the decision making. Through familiarity, her daughters and son-in-law were naturally inclined to follow her lead. Given John McCourtney's background in mechanics and carpentry, he was most likely instrumental in the outfitting and maintenance of the company's equipment and wagons. As the emigrant population waited in Missouri, the first test of their mettle would not be long in coming. In the spring a cholera outbreak began in St. Louis. Originating from steamboat passengers calling port at St. Louis, it extended into the crowded, temporary emigrant encampments, killing many and weakening others. The Evoy/McCourtney family was somehow spared the dreaded malady.

In the second week of May, news of favorable trail conditions reached the encampments, and many companies began their westward journey. The estimated thirty thousand to fifty thousand forty-niners who hit the trails in 1849 represented a broad cross section of society.[4] Women represented a small proportion of the overland emigrants of 1849, with some sources stating 3 percent and others estimating up to 15 percent.[5] Family groups traveling with children represented an even smaller proportion. Although many hailed from the frontier states and came from an agrarian background, there were a surprisingly large number of professionals (lawyers, doctors, accountants, and the like) who caught the gold fever and joined the great emigration. To meet the challenges of overland travel, many travelers organized into formal companies for the journey. By traveling this way, they could share resources, find moral support and security, and enjoy the comradery that came with a communal venture. If these companies lasted through to the California goldfields, they might also pool their resources for enterprise and share in the rewards awaiting them in this land of promise.

Upon hitting the trail, the emigrants were for all practical purposes venturing into the unknown. The Evoy/McCourtney group joined a larger emigrant train, and on May 15, 1849, they set off from Independence and left their former life behind.[6] Of the travel arrangements Bridget's granddaughter Jane later wrote, "Two of Mrs. McCourtney's children were quite small and were placed in [saddle] bags on either side of one of the mules, and if I recall the mule was guided by Mother's [Ellen's] youngest brother

James [Evoy]." Margaret's children, Mary Ann and James, were merely toddlers.[7] Bridget, the seasoned equestrian, rode her white mare sidesaddle, as was customary for women of the era. Ellen also rode on horseback. Margaret, who was experiencing physical frailty at the time, rode in the wagon. Twenty-three-year-old John Evoy (Bridget's eldest son) opted to advance on foot as a "packer," joining the many other travelers anxious to get the goldfields as soon as possible. Swept away in the surging tide of argonauts, he would not be heard from for a few years. On their second day out, May 16, and unbeknownst to them, a major fire broke out in St. Louis, engulfing the city. The conflagration consumed a significant portion of the city and destroyed fifteen city blocks of infrastructure along the riverfront, along with twenty-three steamboats.[8] But isolated on the trail, the family could not know that swathes of their former city lay in ruin.

Traveling with children naturally brought an unpredictability that could hinder the pace of movement for the train. Caring for their practical and emotional needs and dealing with injury and illness was an all-consuming responsibility for mothers. The slow pace of travel would have been frustrating to some who might resent that others, unencumbered with families, would surely get to the goldfields ahead of them.

It was generally understood that there would be scant equipment or tools available for purchase in California and, therefore, most travelers overpacked. The accoutrement of the typical overland traveler and prospective gold miner included cast iron cookware, tools, livestock tack, spare wagon axles and wheels, saws, harvesting scythes, picks and shovels, and of course the essential tool of the miner, gold pans. Many emigrants also packed the tools of their trade so that they could return to their former livelihoods if their fortunes in the goldfields didn't pan out, so to speak. Consequently, some emigrants carried tools for blacksmithing or carpentry and farming implements. One enterprising family traveled with a well-stocked chicken coop mounted to the back of their wagon, no doubt an eternal temptation for others struggling with hunger pangs. Travelers eventually realized that hauling large amounts of cargo by wagon many hundreds of miles over the rugged western landscape was impractical. Many of these belongings would become fodder for the trailside and a seeming windfall for other scavengers, who would likewise eventually abandon many of them farther down the trail. The trailside litter mentioned in diarists' journals included iron stoves, furniture, personal libraries, law book collections, musical instruments, and more. The realities of overland travel soon forced the emigrants to adopt a hard-nosed pragmatism.

The opening weeks of travel took the emigrants northwestward into the Upper Mississippi River basin and across the Great Plains province. In the period after 1825, the Mississippi was conceived as the dividing line between "civilization" and so-called Indian Territory, a zone to which Native Americans would eventually be forcibly removed.[9] Thus, in the Anglo mind, this was a vast, unsettled wilderness filled with potentially life-threatening challenges. Throughout the early nineteenth century, Euro-Americans and Europeans, largely traders, trappers, and various military expeditions, had been venturing into Indian Territory, albeit on a limited scale. Westward expansion via the Oregon Trail began in earnest in the 1840s.[10] Yet, the great migration of 1849 was a sudden influx of tens of thousands of emigrants into areas that, for thousands of years, had been the realm of Indigenous peoples. These Euromerican interlopers generally viewed the Native inhabitants of the American West through a lens colored by ignorance and xenophobia. Through this racial bias, the youthful and imaginative emigrant might anticipate encounters that could lead to narrow escapes from ambushes, violent clashes, or their own heroic exploits in escaping the Indians. In reality, the actual threat toward emigrants was much less than was portrayed in the popular literature of the nineteenth century.[11] Countering the notion of a significant Indian threat, historian John Unruh's research revealed that in the decade between 1850 and 1860, approximately 360 emigrants were killed on the Overland Trail by

Native peoples compared with 425 Indians killed by emigrants.[12] Writing in the context of Nevada, historian Richard Clemmer noted:

> It should be evident that in the gamut of hardships, Indians by no means posed the greatest hazard faced by emigrants along the Humboldt. There were some unfriendly encounters; some poaching by Indians; some poaching by emigrants; some mutual assistance; some mutual hostility. At no time is there any "state of siege" between Indians and emigrants, and at no time are "Indian hostilities" accorded the status of other hardships such as environmental obstacles and disease in diary records.[13]

In the opening few years of the Gold Rush, many Native peoples interacted with the Euro-Americans peacefully, even as some clashed with neighboring tribes. Some Natives traded, others served as trail guides, helped round up stray stock animals, or operated ferrying operations at river crossings. Emigrant diarists describe instances of seemingly curious Indians gathered on the fringes of emigrants' camps and either remaining as silent observers or accepting the invitation to join them for a meal. Likewise, Indigenous people were sometimes willing to give or trade food items to emigrants.[14] Through these interactions the Native peoples could obtain exotic material goods, weapons, or horses. However, and tragically, these interactions also exposed Natives to diseases against which they had no immunity. This, along with a broader process of displacement following the Indian Removal Act of 1830, was transformative for the Native peoples throughout the trans-Mississippi West and set in motion events that would dramatically impact their cultures, their ways of life, and their prospects for survival as distinct ethnic groups.

To guide their westering movement, the Evoy/McCourtney train followed the major rivers that drained the northern plains: the Missouri River as well as the Platte River and its forks, including the Kansas River and the Blue River. These watersheds provided a natural causeway through what became northern Kansas and Nebraska. The Great Plains presented the travelers with several months of monotony and a mundane prelude to their journey. People traveling along this segment of the trail may have been lulled into the belief that this relatively easy travel represented the larger overland experience. This illusion would be shattered soon enough. By the time wagon trains reached Fort Kearny in Nebraska, many travelers were realizing the necessity of lightening their cargo to spare their beasts of burden and hence engaged in wholesale shedding of possessions. Others stubbornly held on to their worldly goods, maintaining the belief that they would reach the promised land with all their chattel intact. Still others were concluding that the trip was more than they had bargained for and turned back toward their former homelands. The equipment and supplies littering the trailside were free for the taking by those backtracking to Missouri.

At the end of each travel day, the important work of making camp and feeding the group was largely the responsibility of the women in the train. While the men drove the animals to forage and water, and cut grass (if present), the women checked in with one another about how they were faring and attended to those with aliments or illness. Each night, after securing the camp and checking on the animals, the Evoy women slept in a tent with Margaret's children. Each morning, irrespective of weather, the breaking of camp started around dawn's first light. Once a fire was started using greasewood brush or buffalo manure, a quick meal was prepared, usually the ubiquitous hardtack biscuit and coffee, and occasionally, bacon or dried beef.

The continuous overland travel exacted an increasing toll on the draft animals, not to mention the emigrants themselves. Writing about the endless toil, forty-niner diarist Catherine Haun noted, "When the going got harder, when oxen and mules failed under the strain with increasing frequency, and the value of every ounce of cargo had to be weighed, then women and children tumbled out and trudged along, mile after mile, day after day."[15] For the Evoy/McCourtney family, the fact of traveling with young children certainly brought unique challenges and considerations. Children could quickly get into mischief, wander off, or be subjected to danger in an instant, especially with skittish draft animals around. Yet, the presence of families likely had positive influences as well. Catherine Haun, who also traveled with a young family noted:

> Our caravan had a good many women and children and although we were probably longer on the journey owing to their presence—they exerted a good influence, as the men did not take such risks with Indians and thereby avoided conflict; were more alert about the care of the teams and seldom had accidents; more attention was paid to cleanliness and sanitation and, lastly but not of less importance, the meals were more regular and better cooked thus preventing much sickness and there was less waste of food.[16]

Many travelers refrained from travel on the Sabbath and engaged in religious observance. On Sundays the devout Evoy and McCourtney families would certainly have engaged in some informal religious service. These breaks allowed for resting and caring for the animals, provisioning, and socializing with other travelers. As Haun noted, "the men were generally busy mending wagons, harnesses, yokes, shoeing the animals, etc. while the wemon [sic] washed clothes, boiled a big mess of beans, to be warmed for several meals, or perhaps mended clothes, if we had devotional service, the minister pro-tem stood at the center of the corral while we all kept on with our work."[17] Sometimes the women reached out to female travelers from other families to offer support and maintain a sense of normalcy, particularly for the young children. One young mother noted in her diary:

During the day we womenfolk visited from wagon to wagon or congenial friends spent an hour walking, ever westward, and talking over our home life back in 'the states'; telling of the loved ones left behind; voicing our hopes for the future in the far west and even whispering a little friendly gossip of emigrant life. High teas were not popular but tatting, knitting, crocheting [sic], exchanging receipts for cooking beans or dried apples or swopping food for the sake of variety kept us in practice of feminine occupations and diversions. We did not keep late hours but when not too engrossed with fear of the red enemy or dread of impending danger we enjoyed the hour around the campfire.[18]

Haun likewise described a typical scene around the nightly campfire: "The menfolk lolling and smoking their pipes and guessing, or maybe betting, how many miles we had covered during the day. We listened to readings, story-telling, music and songs and the day often ended in laughter and merrymaking."[19]

Although the Evoy/McCourtney family members did not keep diaries on the journey, other travelers did, and their entries offer some insight about the conditions and challenges that the family experienced in their daily toil along the trail. The first evidence of the group's progress on the Overland Trail comes through the writings of a fellow emigrant Hugh Heiskell, from Tennessee. On July 29, the Tennessean and his wagon train camped with the Evoy/McCourtney train at Greasewood Creek, a tributary of the Sweetwater River and one of the few locations where travelers could obtain water on the four-day journey between the Platte and Sweetwater Rivers.[20] Heiskell's train would meet up with the Evoy train on more than one occasion, and Heiskell mentioned John McCourtney in several journal entries.[21] Heiskell's company was lucky enough to be guided by Charles Taplin, a veteran of two of John C. Frémont's previous expeditions to the California Territory. Serving as principal guide for Frémont, Taplin had made Sierran crossings and traversed the interior of California during a particularly harrowing expedition in 1848–49.[22] While camped together, Taplin and Heiskell struck up a friendship with McCourtney. This interaction would likely have given the Evoy/McCourtney group intelligence on the Sierran routes, and more broadly, the diverse geography they would have to traverse. Another well-known emigrant company traveling within a few days of the Evoy/McCourtney train was that of Joseph Goldsborough Bruff, whose writings and sketches of his Gold Rush experiences are often cited by writers of the California Trail genre.[23] Additionally, another prominent forty-niner and diarist, William Swain of the Wolverine Rangers emigrant company, traveled the same trail segments, usually within two to five days of Bridget's group. The journals and letters of these fellow travelers documenting their daily progress provides insight into the movements and experiences of the Evoy/McCourtney train in the same time frame.

It was in this section of the overland route that emigrants might encounter bands of Blackfeet (Aamsskáápipikani or Southern Pikuni) and/or Crow (Absaroka) Natives. These groups were generally considered by neighboring peoples as the most warlike in the region.[24] Like most Euro-Americans, the Evoys and McCourtneys were probably imbued with the portrayal of Native Americans as savages and may have been anxious at the prospect of an encounter. In fact, the family's first encounter with Native men on the trail turned out to be benign, perhaps even helpful. This incident may have occurred in the Platte River section of The Overland Trail in Wyoming. The emigrant rumor mill told of a stretch of forest about ten miles long where they might encounter a tribe that was reportedly openly hostile to emigrants. Bridget's granddaughter Jane later recorded the following story, told to her by her mother, Ellen:

> Just as Grandmothers' [Bridget's] train was entering the forest—an Indian Chief arrayed in all his trappings rode up to mother's [Ellen's] side—and rode with her all

through the Forest. Just as they emerged from the forest the Indian put spurs into his horse and galloped away. Mother said that she had given the Indian a Rosary and other trinkets and she supposed she had won his friendship and protection.[25]

Although not mentioned in this quotation, the chief was most likely accompanied by at least a few other men of the tribe. They may have belonged to the Crow people who lived within that region on the plains.[26] That he focused his attention on Bridget and Ellen, who were at the head of the column on horseback, suggests that he may have viewed them as leading the wagon train. Crow social structure was both matrilineal and matriarchal, so women played significant roles and held important responsibilities within tribal society.[27] Some Crow women became adept in horseback riding and hunting, and some even served as warriors, joining the men in war parties and engaging in battle.[28] Perhaps most significantly, the Evoy women and their companions could not have anticipated the attitude or intentions of the chief and his men in this encounter. Upon seeing the Natives, Bridget and Ellen may have moved to the front of the train in order to set a nonthreatening tone for the encounter. That Ellen would relinquish her rosary, an important article of her religion, suggests her great anxiety.

After departing Greasewood Creek, Wyoming, the Evoy/McCourtney group crossed the Continental Divide at South Pass, the halfway point between the Missouri gateway settlements and the Californian goldfields and a symbolic waypoint noted by many diarists. Just eighteen miles west of South Pass, the group reached an important landmark for travelers: the first major fork in the trail, called the "Parting of the Ways." The northern fork continued along the traditional trail toward the Oregon Territory, the southern one (the Fort Bridger Road) led to several additional forks, all of which purportedly led to California but some of which traversed punishing terrain that was impassible for wagons. One

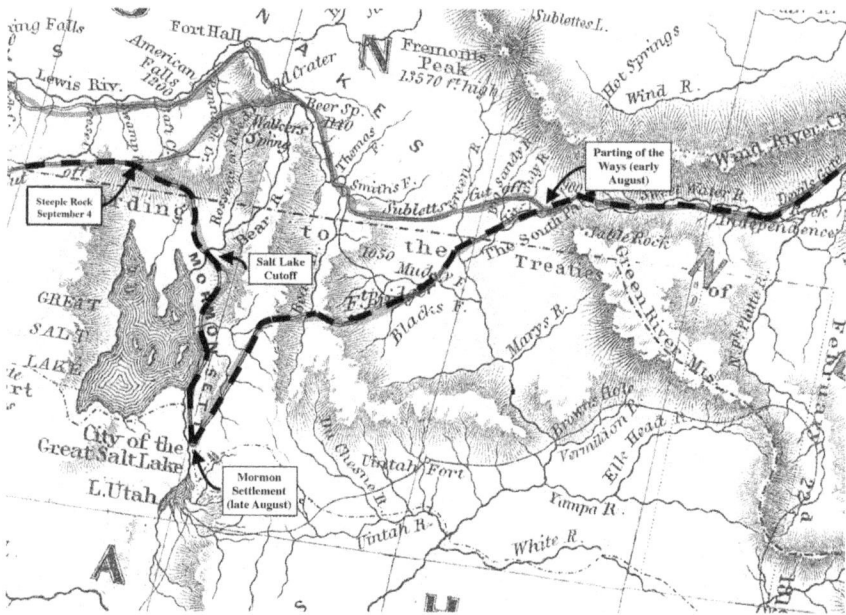

Map showing the principal routes within the central portion of the Overland Trail. Courtesy of the David Rumsey Map Collection, David Rumsey Map Center, Stanford University Libraries.

of those alternate forks, Hastings Cutoff, led to the recent Mormon settlement at Salt Lake. Shared trail intelligence suggested that travelers could replenish their supplies and obtain fresh livestock there. Due to the degraded condition of their stock and dwindling supplies, the Evoy/McCourtney train decided to take a chance on this significant detour to Salt Lake, as did about one-third of the emigrant trains that year.[29]

Passing several trail forks or "cutoffs," the Evoy/McCourtney train followed what appeared to be the most heavily traveled trails toward Salt Lake. During this time, the Mormons were struggling in their isolated settlement within the Great Basin. Drought, hard frosts, and insect infestation had led to back-to-back crop failures. The six thousand residents at the settlement had barely survived these hardships.[30] The interactions between the Mormons and emigrants calling on the settlement were generally positive and often mutually beneficial. Through these visits, the Mormons bartered for much-needed supplies, while the forty-niners received food (including vegetables) and fresh livestock at a crucial point in their journey.[31] Many emigrant visitors to the settlement probably welcomed the opportunity to part with unwanted equipment through barter or sale and obtain foodstuffs or fresh livestock as well.

At nearly the same time as the Evoy/McCourtney train was approaching the Salt Lake Valley, two independent government-sponsored groups with their respective military escorts were entering the area: those of General John Wilson and Captain Howard Stansbury. Wilson, the newly appointed Indian agent for the California Territory, was on his way to a new post at the burgeoning city of San Francisco. Captain Howard Stansbury and his company, who were being guided by the venerable mountain man Jim Bridger were conducting a survey of the territory with the idea of establishing a railroad route through the region.[32] Tensions between the Mormons and the federal government had been simmering over issues ranging from governance and landownership to the controversial custom of plural marriage. Hence, the sudden arrival of the two government trains so soon after the establishment of the Mormon settlement appeared somewhat ominous to the community elders. In fact, Stansbury later acknowledged, "I was told that they [the Mormon leaders] would not permit any survey of their country to be made; while it was starkly hinted that if I persevered in attempting to carry it on, my life would scarce be safe."[33] It was against this background of elevated tensions that the Evoy/McCourtney train entered the settlement.

At Salt Lake, the Evoy/McCourtney group camped for five days. They had friendly relations with some of the local settlers and, despite their disparate religious affiliations and customs, they found kindred spirits. Perhaps they found common ground with the Mormons in the shared value of family. They rested the teams, purchased provisions, and replaced some of their oxen. On meeting the group at the main California Trail two weeks later,

Hugh Heiskell received a description of the settlement from John McCourtney: "Their city has one thousand houses, the products of agriculture are abundant, for which the emigrants pay a high price—for instance $16 for one hundred pounds of flour. Green corn, potatoes, & other vegetables plenty, also watermelons."[34] This brief respite allowed the group to rest and gather their strength, while the McCourtney children could perhaps play with other children at the tent city settlement. After becoming friendly with a young Mormon woman, Ellen offered her a jar of strawberry jam that inexplicably had survived temptation over three months of overland travel, a luxury indeed.[35] Of this stay, Jane Montgomery later wrote:

> At Salt Lake Mother [Ellen] and a Mormon woman became quite friendly, which proved to be very fortunate. Grandmother's party, after deliberating had decided to take the Southern Route to California. That night Mother was awakened by the flap of her tent being raised—and her Mormon friend tiptoed to her side—with her fingers to her lips said "Don't go by the Southern Route. Don't tell anyone I told you or I'll be killed."[36]

The unidentified woman was presumably aware of rumors about potential violence directed at emigrants who ventured into the southerly reaches of their territory. Given the unwanted intrusion of government-led groups into the area, there may have been a will among some of the Mormon leadership to thwart further excursions toward the south. Directly following this encounter, Ellen pulled her mother aside and discreetly told her of the unnerving conversation. Torn between her loyalty to the larger emigrant company and a moral obligation to protect the well-being of these new friends, Bridget handled the dilemma decisively. Jane continued, "in the morning Grandmother announced that she had decided to take the Northern Route and invited as many as cared—to join her party. But there was a difference of opinion—and the party split up—some preferred to take the Southern Route."[37]

In wresting a leadership role from the male contingent of the train, Bridget's message was clear: those who followed her would have to accept her leadership. She had symbolically placed a fork in the road and pointed to the path forward. Their original train was now reduced to probably no more than several dozen travelers and their wagons. Although restocking and obtaining fresh oxen had given them much-needed relief, the Salt Lake Valley side trip had cost them crucial travel time crossing the Basin and Range Province. This delay would bring grave consequences for the group.

CHAPTER 3

Running the Gauntlet

Death, the great leveler, respecting neither age, gender, or station, assured women's full participation as observers, victims, and bereaved in this too-familiar gold rush experience.

JoAnn Levy, "They Saw the Elephant"

The momentous decision at Salt Lake over, Bridget raised her hand signaling her readiness to start, reined in her mare for an about-face to the north, and led the group on an alternate route, the Salt Lake Cutoff. Established by Samuel J. Hensley in the previous year, this 180-mile detour skirted the east side of the lake, thereby avoiding the worst of the dreaded Salt Lake Desert. The train set off on a week of hard travel through the rugged, barren terrain and, under pressure to pick up the pace of travel, they chose not to halt on the Sabbath, a very unusual omission for the devout Catholics.[1] This decision speaks volumes about pace of travel being their priority. Each night, while waiting for sleep to come, Bridget may have wondered if she had made the right decision in choosing the northerly route. At the time she knew nothing of the fate of the southerly bound splinter group. Years later in California, Bridget would run into a member of this group. This man (whose name was not recorded) relayed that his group had been ambushed en route by men disguised as Indians.[2] He was the sole survivor of the attack.

In the immediate moment, however, taking the northerly route required crossing the rugged Raft River Mountains as well as fording watercourses including the Bear River. After a week of travel in this brutal landscape, the group rejoined the California Trail at Steeple Rock (City of Rocks) in present-day Idaho. Once again they were traveling within a few days of the Wolverine Rangers and even closer to Hugh Heiskell and his company. In fact, Heiskell's group encountered Bridget's train at Goose Creek, a tributary of the Humboldt River, five weeks after having last seen them at Greasewood Creek, Wyoming, prior to their taking the Hastings Cutoff trail variant toward Salt Lake. At Goose Greek on September 4, Heiskell noted in his diary:

> At noon McCourtney's train—with two ladies [presumably Bridget and Ellen Evoy]—were below us on the creek, the same that camped with us Sunday, July 29, on Greasewood Creek [Wyoming], where our oxen were first affected by the alkali. They came via Salt Lake & gave a favorable account of the flourishing condition of the Mormons. . . . [Mc]Courtney beat us a little, we entering the cut-off as he passed, but he only lay by [stayed] 5 days & purchased fresh cattle at Salt Lake.[3]

Travelers greatly dreaded the Basin and Range segment of the trail, especially the Humboldt Sink, which they generally understood as wasteland with very poor forage and rare water sources. The soil contained concentrations of alkalis, fine caustic salts such as lime or soda, which the teams kicked up, enflaming the noses, eyes, and throats of people and stock animals. It was especially toxic in water sources, a situation responsible for the illness and death of thousands of stock animals and severe illnesses among the travelers who drank the water. The aching thirst of both emigrants and beasts was made all the worse by an endless trek through ankle-deep, hot volcanic dust, which formed a blanket across the valley bottoms. Bridget, Ellen, and Margaret may well have tried to reassure the children that these hardships were only temporary and that things would be better if they could just reach the next summit, river crossing, camping spot, or grassy meadow. In the expansive Basin and Range, these imagined waypoints were often reached days after they were needed.

Of this trail segment historian Richard Clemmer wrote vividly: "The Humboldt Trail constituted a disagreeable gamut of endurance tests that strained emigrants' degrees of self-possession and sense of identity; by the time they reached it, they must have realized that they were not merely following along in the pioneer spirit, but rather, that they had unwittingly challenged themselves to a duel with unknown forces."[4] There was no relief from the infernal heat and sun in this treeless expanse. In the Great Basin, exposure and lack of potable water were the killers. Touching on this point, a traveler by the name of Niles Searles who was journeying along the same trail in the same time frame as the Evoys declared, "the thermometer indicates 140 [degrees] on this arid plain." Another diarist recorded a daytime temperature of 105 degrees, which was undoubtedly more accurate than Searles's reading. Nevertheless, Searles's description evokes the experience of crossing this "arid burning waste." Bernard J. Reid, another emigrant traveling on the same trail at that time lamented "Beneath the merciless sun, the whole atmosphere glows like an oven. . . . Off to the southwest, as far as the eye can extend, nothing appears but a level desert. . . . this we must cross."[5]

Struggling through hot sand, dust storms, and oppressive heat within the vast Humboldt Basin, the Evoy/McCourtney still had to face the final barrier in their journey, the Sierras. Spanish for "snowy range," the Sierra Nevada mountain range was so named by the Franciscan missionary Padre Pedro Font, who in 1776 noted the rugged mountains during his trek through Alta California. The tragedy of the Donner Party, who became snowbound and were trapped in the mountains' wintery grip for months, had played out only two years prior in 1847 and served as a grim reminder of the consequences of consuming too much time and resources en route to the Sierras. Those who tarried in the Great Basin did so at great peril. As the month of September drew to a close, a battle of attrition was being waged in the Basin and Range, and survival emerged as *the* focus for those still crossing the desert. The family and their overland comrades were all too aware that somewhere just beyond the horizon, the formidable "snowy range" awaited them. As they drew nearer, the anticipation of that encounter taunted them in the daytime and haunted their anxious nights. To survive the final obstacle of their journey, emigrants would need to summon whatever tenacity and mental toughness they held in reserve. For many that would not be enough.

As Bridget's train moved through the Humboldt Basin, they were met with rumors and grim descriptions of the situation at Truckee Meadows, a crucial waypoint on the Truckee and Carson routes, the traditional target trails through the Sierras. Rumors circulating about depleted grazing areas and a scant water supply at the meadows were particularly distressing, as this was the last opportunity for forage before the traverse of the high Sierran passes. Incidentally, a new fork in the trail had been established east of Truckee Meadows, called variously Lassen's Cutoff, Lassen's Trail, Lawson's Route, the Lassen Road, the Northern Route, or more sarcastically, the "Greenhorn Cutoff."[6] This trail had been pioneered by Peter Lassen in the previous year. Having heard about the rumored difficulties on the Truckee Route, many trains took Lassen's Cutoff in the belief they could avoid the highest mountain passes, have a better chance of obtaining pasturage en route, and shorten their mileage over the Sierras significantly. These misapprehensions would lead to terrific hardship for all and tragedy for too many.

Bridget and company, aware that their oxen had been greatly weakened during the punishing trek out of the Salt Lake Valley, experienced growing anxiety as they approached the Sierras, with its stark peaks glinting on the horizon. While camped at the fork of the main trail at Lassen's Cutoff on September 27, Heiskell once again encountered the Evoy/McCourtney group, noting in his journal: "Just below where we are camped the south Oregon Road [Lassen's route] leads off. Taplin and the Colonel were down there at 5 o'clock this evening and saw McCourtney there, and his train moving on. He [McCourtney] came in at Steeple Rock with fresh cattle from the Salt Lake and had traveled every Sunday."[7]

At the Lassen trailhead, McCourtney spoke with Heiskell about the group's intentions. Heiskell explained, "His cattle are broke down. He says they cannot pull up hill of any steepness, & for that reason he takes the road [Lassen's Cutoff] to avoid the mountain."[8] Other emigrants entering the cutoff just one week ahead of Bridget's group included the trains of J. Goldsborough Bruff (eight days earlier), William Swain and Dr. Joseph Middleton of the Wolverine Rangers (six days earlier), Dr. Israel Lord, Rebecca Foster Reeve and two brothers Clayton and Robert, and Catherine Haun.[9] Their proximity meant these groups occasionally camped at the same place only a day or few days apart. The contemporaneous writings of Bruff, Swain, Middleton, Haun, Henry L. Ford, and Reeve offered insight, in real time, into the experiences that the Evoy/McCourtney group encountered on the Lassen Route. Rebecca Reeve later joined a larger group that included the Evoy/McCourtney families.[10]

In fact, Lassen's Cutoff actually added considerable mileage to the overland journey and coursed through a desolate landscape that afforded precious little relief from thirst, hunger and exposure.[11] The consequences of committing their trains to this "shortcut" would not become clear until the emigrants had already paid too high a price to justify reversing course, for they were truly "riding the back of the tiger." Once fully committed, men and women alike would have to persevere or perish. Of this predicament the historian JoAnn Levy wrote: "Death, the great leveler, respecting neither age, gender, or station, assured women's full participation as observers, victims, and bereaved in this all too familiar gold rush experience."[12] The first of several daunting challenges was crossing the Black Rock Desert, 300,000 acres of sunbaked, dry lakebed, one of the largest flat surfaces on earth. The furnace-like effect of the basin and lack of potable water and forage in this hellish desertscape dealt a fatal blow to the remaining livestock, and to some extent, the emigrants themselves. To escape the worst of the heat, many groups traveled at night and escaped the relentless sun by sleeping under their wagons during the middle of the day (if they still had a wagon). The remarkably flat ground surface often produced mirages of water-filled basins, inexplicably shimmering on the otherwise scorched desert floor. Oxen stampeded toward these mirages, expending what little energy they had left. Very rare sources of water were available, save for a few well-known and over-tapped sources such as Antelope Springs and Rabbit Hole Springs. Some stock animals, delirious and exhausted, collapsed into watering holes, drowning and contaminating the springs, thereby eliminating them as a source of water for future passersby. With the large-scale loss of livestock came the inevitable abandonment of more trappings and supplies, as well as wagons. This meant the path forward would be on foot for many. Among these challenges was the harsh reality of the high death toll exacted on the emigrants from illness, exposure, and injury. In his diary J. Goldsborough Bruff mentions encountering an average of one or two gravesites per day of travel in this section of the trail, which ranged between twelve and twenty miles.[13] Neither human nor beast was immune from the Grim Reaper. For these and other reasons, the sinister monikers "Lassen's Death Route" and "Trail of Death" soon emerged in the lexicon of the 1849 emigration.[14] Whether by luck or through good husbandry Bridget's train managed to preserve their gaunt oxen and therefore survive this seemingly apocalyptic landscape. After crossing the Black Rock Desert, they would have to traverse the High Rock Canyon region which, although beautiful, presented a confounding labyrinth of canyons and jagged ridges. Once out of the High Rock Canyon, the eastern escarpment of the Warner Mountains awaited them, and just to the west, the storied California Territory.

By mid-September 1849 the lead elements of the overland emigration began arriving in the Sacramento Valley, but the collective

migration extended several hundred miles back into the Humboldt Basin, where thousands had yet to enter the Sierras. Some
of these travelers had traversed the Truckee Route, which took
them by the former encampments of the ill-fated Donner Party
at Alder Creek and Donner Lake.[15] As they trudged passed the
collapsed log lean-tos and nondescript debris and bones strewn
about the ground at the Donner encampments, these travelers
were, no doubt, reminded of the ultimate price to be paid for getting caught in the Sierras so late in the season. Whether the bones
were human or animal didn't matter, their very sight inspired a vis-
ceral reaction—revulsion. Other travelers emerging from Lassen's
Cutoff into the Sacramento Valley described the acute challenges
of this ill-conceived, longer route. As more emigrants arrived and
shared intelligence on their experiences with the trail, it became
clear that a significant number of emigrants would be entering
the mountains at the onset of winter. Most of these people were
completely unprepared for mountain weather. Struggling with
the cumulative impacts of fatigue and illness, minimal food, and
failing livestock, these travelers were unknowing participants in a
large-scale humanitarian disaster.

The military and civilian authorities in the California Territory foresaw tragedy on a scale that would make the Donner Party
legacy pale by orders of magnitude. As an immediate response,
General Persifor F. Smith, the military governor of California,
ordered the military authorities to initiate a rescue operation
and approved the release of federal funds to finance the effort.[16]
An advance of $100,000 in credit was issued by the government
with additional contributions offered by prominent citizens.[17]
Smith's subordinate, Brevet Major Daniel H. Rucker, quickly
organized a relief effort. Although needed resources were spread
far and wide within the territory, Rucker quickly arranged for the
hiring of experienced teamsters and the purchase of food, livestock, and wagons for the relief effort.[18] His "government men,"
or "Relief Company" as they were commonly called, traversed the
primary routes of emigration over the Sierras (Carson's Route,

Truckee Pass Route, and Lassen's Cutoff). In the course of this mission, they distributed resources, shared updated trail information, implored the emigrants to shed unnecessary cargo, and when needed, rescued emigrants in distress. Based on fresh trail intelligence coming from recently arrived packers, General Smith and Major Rucker soon realized that Lassen's Cutoff presented the direst situation because of Indian activity. The local Indians in the canyons and montane meadows of the Modoc Plateau, and the Pit River watershed in particular, were actively raiding the emigrants' livestock, leaving many no choice but to discard their wagons and much of their belongings. Further advance would be on foot at a point when many could barely walk. Hence, of the three principal routes over the mountains, Lassen's Cutoff was quickly given the highest priority for the rescue mission. Contemporaneous correspondence between leaders of the relief effort, comments by overland diarists, and inferences drawn from the contemporaneous information provides insight on the route, progress, and experiences of the Evoy/McCourtney group in this saga, a story rooted in terrific adversity, tragedy, and a true test of the human spirit.

As the emigrants traversed the high pass over the Warner Mountains and dropped into the Goose Lake Basin, they entered the ancestral lands of the Pit River Tribe. Speaking a language in the Palaihnihan language family, these people comprised eleven autonomous bands that had traditionally occupied the Modoc Plateau, a rugged volcanic landscape in the northeast corner of the California Territory. The Hewisedawi, or Hewise (Hay-wee-see), Band occupied the Goose Lake and the Pit River drainages just beyond the western flank of the Warner Mountain Range.[19] The Atsugewi and Achumawi also shared the Pit River region on the west and south, respectively. Through their traditions and origin stories, the tribes of this area viewed the natural and spiritual worlds as indistinguishable from each another. They were taught by their tribal elders to appreciate and manage the resources available to them and to live within this world in a balanced fashion.

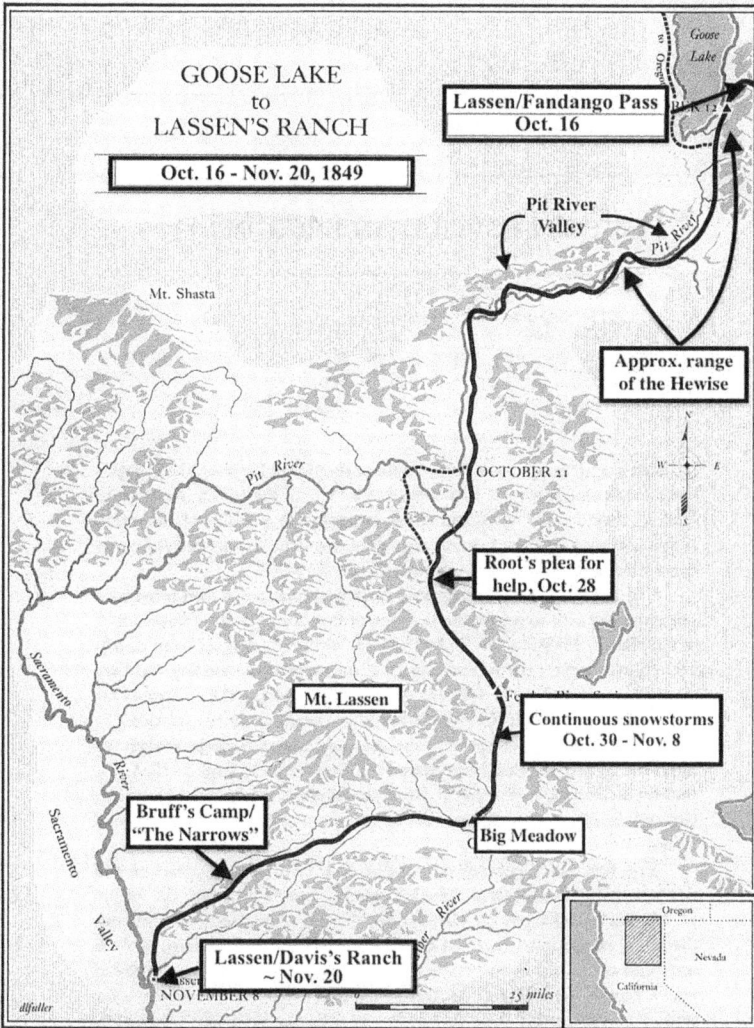

GOOSE LAKE
to
LASSEN'S RANCH

Oct. 16 - Nov. 20, 1849

Lassen/Fandango Pass
Oct. 16

Goose Lake

Pit River
Valley

Pit River

Mt. Shasta

Approx. range
of the Hewise

Pit River

OCTOBER 21

N
W   E
S

Root's plea for
help, Oct. 28

Mt. Lassen

Continuous snowstorms
Oct. 30 - Nov. 8

Sacramento

River

Bruff's Camp/
"The Narrows"

Sacramento

Big Meadow

Valley

Lassen/Davis's Ranch
~ Nov. 20

NOVEMBER 8

25 miles

dlfuller

Oregon

Nevada

California

The California segment of Lassen's Cutoff where the government-sponsored relief effort was carried out from September to November 1849. Courtesy of the University of Oklahoma Press.

According to seasonal patterns they foraged, hunted, and used what the land provided on a scale and pace that was largely sustainable.[20] Subject to droughts and harsh winters, the Modoc country could be a very difficult place to eke out an existence, and competition with neighboring tribes over resources could become fierce and occasionally lead to conflict between the Pit River and neighboring Yana and Modoc Natives.[21]

By late October the fish runs on the Pit River were flagging, and the larger game were migrating toward the lower foothills in anticipation of winter. The chill in the air and the first morning frosts signaled that winter was imminent. During these lean months the Native peoples would be dependent on cached food stocks, which were not always enough to relieve their hunger. The sudden influx of hundreds of emigrants tramping through their territory was undoubtedly a profoundly unsettling experience. The cacophony of their trains and their probing hunters tended to drive the remaining game out of the immediate area, which did not bode well for the Native men who were particularly keen on acquiring meat late in the season when its availability waned. In the Modoc country, the appearance of abundant livestock on the Lassen Trail provided the Hewise a windfall of food, and perhaps horses, but attempting to acquire it would come at a price.[22] Their knowledge of the geography and terrain combined with their tracking skills gave the Hewise every advantage. In preparation for nighttime raids on emigrants' livestock, Native men would gather in groups on the ridges waiting for dark, the men keeping in communication via signal fires. Unprepared and outmatched in this cunning game, the emigrants learned to dread the sight of the signal fires, which implied they would be pulling another all-nighter standing guard. The Native men either drove the livestock off the main trail where they could butcher the animals at their leisure, or they dispatched the animals upon sight so that they could obtain the meat under cover of darkness. Highly valued by the Indigenous peoples, horses were driven off and adopted.

Meanwhile, Major Rucker initially put a civilian, John H. Peoples, in charge of a relief train intended for Lassen's Cutoff.

After further refection, Rucker joined the effort personally and led a second relief company up trail. John Peoples's actions would prove he had the mental toughness and discipline needed to carry out this daunting task.[23] Peoples hired several civilians with livestock ranging experience as teamsters to assist in driving stock up the Lassen Trail, among them Elisha H. Todd and Henry L. Ford, both of whom would prove their mettle in the relief effort. Their names, along with those of Peoples and Rucker, would later become prominent in the retelling of the historic "government relief effort" of 1849. After procuring the necessary manpower, livestock, wagons, and food (flour, bread, pork, and especially beef on the hoof) to mount these rescue/relief efforts, Peoples, and shortly thereafter Rucker, traversed the Lassen Trail northeastward against the direction of emigration. The execution of this rescue effort required tenacity and terrific endurance. Traveling under very difficult trail conditions, this relief mission required repeated multiday traverses up and down the rugged trail, dispensing food, fending off impossible requests for supplies and livestock, and all the while dealing with the Indian raiding and its damage to the struggling travelers. There were no resources to provide medical treatment, save for the odd doctor who might also be afflicted with illness or, more likely, malnutrition. When encountering groups of emigrants, Rucker and his assistants typically dispatched a cow, quartered it, and distributed the raw beef among them. In some instances, they simply hung cuts of beef in trailside trees, knowing the emigrants would take what they found—if bears, mountain lions, or birds of prey didn't get to it first. Such was the grim business of survival on Lassen's Cutoff. Upon penetrating the northerly reaches of the trail, Peoples and his hired assistants made the descent into the Pit River Valley from the south and soon attracted the attention of the Hewise. Here they shifted between giving aid to emigrants while also engaging the Indian men in skirmishes and fending off nighttime raids. Dead stock animals lined the trails, some bristling with arrows, others torn asunder by predators. With the onset of winter looming and many travelers battling debilitating illness, verging on starvation, and losing animals to exhaustion or raiding, the emigrants at the tail end of the migration faced a perfect storm of adversity.

Under orders from Major Rucker to travel to the end of the trail of emigrants just east of the Warner Mountain Range, Captain Elisha Todd was tasked with offering aid and providing travelers with important intelligence on the arduous mountain crossing through the rugged Modoc and Sierran country.[24] On October 12, Captain Todd encountered the Wolverine Rangers camped near the summit of the Warner Range at Lassen Pass and offered a stark assessment of the upcoming trail. Joseph Pratt, a member of the company, paraphrased Captain Todd when he wrote in his journal, "It is useless for us to try to get our teams through." Pratt added, "We should hurry on for our lives."[25] Todd's admonition had an immediate impact on the Rangers who, up to this point, had shown considerable discipline and fortitude in dealing with hardships on The Overland Trail. On the following day they called a company meeting and formally disbanded, a signal that from this point onward, the order of the day was "every man for himself." Like most of the emigrants, the Rangers had assumed that the Warner Mountains were part of the Sierra Nevada range and that, once over the pass, they would soon be in the Sacramento Valley. But the views from the pass revealed a broad expanse of jagged ridges, narrow canyons and conical-shaped volcanic peaks that comprised the Modoc Plateau. Inexplicably, while lingering at the pass, William Swain and his Wolverine Ranger comrades, along with other travelers, held an impromptu celebration with dancing and music (a fandango) that evening of the fourteenth in the mistaken belief they had finally breached the last significant obstacle of the overland journey.[26] The celebration inspired the moniker later given to the location, "Fandango Pass."[27]

Meanwhile, somewhere within the rugged high desert terrain east of the Warner Range, fear gripped the Evoy/McCourtney group as they grappled with the rapid failure of their oxen. Their belongings and supplies, crucial for getting through the mountains, would soon have to be abandoned, perhaps even before they breached the mountain pass. Due to this unfolding situation,

John McCourtney made the agonizing decision to break free of the group and forge ahead on foot as a "packer" in hopes of obtaining provisions and with luck a mule or two. After a few weeks' travel on foot, he intended to backtrack to the family train. He had difficult discussions with Margaret and Bridget, but ultimately, with their crucial support, the decision was made: he would leave them and beat a path to the first source of assistance he could find. Somewhere east of the Warner Range, he said his farewells and began his trek up the Warner escarpment. While crossing over the summit, McCourtney may have crossed paths with Captain Todd and been told that he could obtain provisions at the government encampment in Feather River Valley, several days' journey down trail. He most likely told Todd about the expected arrival of the family train, which he believed to be a few days travel behind him. As the last of the stragglers arrived at the pass, however, there were no signs of Bridget's group. It was clear that something was amiss. Todd and a few assistants traversed down the eastern slope of the Warner Range to find them and any others left behind. Family oral tradition provides clarity on the group's delay. Jane Montgomery (paraphrasing Ellen) later recalled that the family train "came to a fork in the road. They were puzzled as to which road to take." After due deliberation they took what appeared to be the most feasible route. This trail fork led in a full day of travel through rugged terrain. This may well have been in the High Rock Canyon segment of the trail.[28] Jane later recounted, "but after travelling all day, they found they had taken a dead end road which lead [sic] to a high mountain. Discouraged and disheartened the men leaned against the wall and wept like children."[29]

Lost in a labyrinth of deep canyons and ridges, and emotionally spent, the group knew they had wasted precious energy at this crucial point in their push over the last barrier to the valley of the Sacramento. Deeply concerned for group morale, Bridget intervened. As Jane explained: "Grandmother [Bridget] took charge— she ordered dinner prepared—then with renewed courage they retraced their steps and just when they reached the forked road, they met a government train which had been sent to hunt them, as they had been reported lost."[30] Captain Todd and his men offered them what food they could spare, sufficient to stave off the pangs of hunger. The men helped them get their exhausted teams up the escarpment of Lassen Pass, an elevation gain of 1,600 feet in just two miles of travel. This required double-teaming their oxen and frequently chocking the wagon wheels to allow the oxen to "blow hard" and catch their breath.[31] The men and women all joined in this backbreaking and dangerous work. It was not unusual for a wagon to break away on a steep grade and careen wildly down trail, causing injury to people and livestock alike.

Wagon train negotiating rugged terrain in the Basin and Range Province, circa 1869. Collection of the Oakland Museum of California.

Bridget's company crossed Lassen Pass on October 16, essentially among the last group of travelers to cross the summit. As they stood at the mountain pass, gazing over the horizon, they saw not the Sacramento Valley of their dreams, but a sweeping expanse of ridges, valleys, and mountains as far as the eye could see. This panorama comprised three major features of the Pacific Mountain System: the Modoc Plateau in the foreground, the southern Cascade Mountain Range to the north, and the Sierra Nevada to the south. From this vantage point, the Evoy/McCourtney group could see what Swain had described in his journal only a day earlier, "to the west of us, solitary, rises to an immense height, a gigantic mountain [Mt. Shasta], the top and sides clear to the base covered with snow—a magnificent sight."[32] Upon reaching the summit only a day or two earlier, Rebecca Reeve had written similarly: "The view from the sumet was undiscribably beautiful, down into the valley of California lovely with a bordering of pine forest, the finest growth of immence pines, Balsams, and other varieties quite new to us, with the valley clothed with a rich growth of grass looking in the distance so soft and tinted as if the painters brush had passed over it."[33] Through Captain Todd, Bridget's party received reliable intelligence, a rarity on the Overland Trail. The news was soul crushing: The Sacramento Valley (and Lassen's Ranch, or Rancho de Bosquejo) was more than two hundred miles away, requiring a month or more of travel across a vast mountainous terrain. Emphasizing the adversity they faced, Todd added that the road ahead was the "worst in all the world," requiring numerous cold-water river crossings. He further warned that the Pit River Indians were sure to probe into the encampments at night, seeking to drive off the emigrants' livestock, a loss that would quickly end their advance by wagon. Simultaneously, on October 16 or thereabouts, the emigrants were also hearing of the recent death of Captain William Warner and his guide, who were part of a paramilitary group that had been ambushed by unidentified Indians two weeks earlier near Eightmile Creek, a mere dozen miles to the north of the pass.[34] The motive for this ambush was unclear, the Natives may have seen the armed group as a threat or may have been avenging the killing of some of their own people by emigrants. It was clear that some Natives were prepared to defend their territorial range even if it entailed violence against well-armed and disciplined forces.

While at the pass, Bridget's group befriended John K. Root, formerly of the Wolverine Rangers. He reiterated what he had been told of the conditions ahead and perhaps repeated Captain Todd's admonition to purge the wagons and hurry on for their lives. Reeling from the grim news, the Evoy/McCourtney train members hunkered down for the night at the pass. As they sat around the fire and discussed the path forward, a sense of profound dread must have descended on the group. Although they could not know it, about this time Rebecca Reeve's brother Clayton was ambushed and killed by Indians on the Pit River, just down trail (west) of the Evoy/McCourtney group encampment.[35] Unarmed in the wilderness and unable to communicate with his family, John McCourtney passed the location where Reeve had been killed in a fusillade of arrows. McCourtney's absence at this critically important moment was sorely felt. Bridget, Ellen, and Margaret surely helped steady jittery nerves among the group, the children's questions about their father's absence would have to be deflected for the time being. The bite of cold air on the skin and waves of dark clouds blowing in from the west were harbingers of mountain winter weather, as unpredictable as it was unforgiving. As they stirred in the morning and broke camp, all were aware that a labyrinth of terrain and adversity lay between this mountain pass and salvation at the Sacramento Valley. First up, on the near horizon, was the gauntlet presented by the Hewise. To help keep the group motivated on the path forward, Bridget may have projected calm determination, but beyond that she could only pray for their deliverance.

CHAPTER 4

Deliverance

Thousands have laid and will lay their bones along the
routes to and in this country. Tell all that "death is in the pot"
if they attempt to cross the plains and hellish mountains.

William Swain to George Swain, January 6, 1850

While Bridget's group summoned their strength for their descent
into the Goose Lake Basin from Lassen Pass, John McCourtney
was trekking through the Pit River Valley. His goal was the government encampment at East Spring, Feather River Valley, where
he hoped to acquire provisions and perhaps a mule or two to
bring back to his family. While en route McCourtney encountered a small advance party of teamsters heading up trail, led by
John Peoples. Hearing of the dire conditions of the family train,
Peoples promised to provide aid when he encountered them. On
October 18, McCourtney reached Major Rucker's government
camp at East Spring. Rucker provided him and several other packers with rations of beef and bread, but the major had no mules
to spare.[1] John was about ten days' travel down trail of the family
group and, although he had not encountered any Hewise, he was
hearing news of encounters from other travelers and becoming
aware of the threat they posed to the trains. He would have to
backtrack through the dreaded Pit River Valley to return to his
family. At this time, Bridget's group was just entering the opposite end of the Pit River Valley from the north. Anxious days and
sleepless nights were ahead for the families as they attempted to

"run the gauntlet." They could not know of the violent skirmishes between Peoples's men and the Hewise during a probe into the valley just a few weeks earlier. While advancing through the diverse volcanic landscape of the Modoc country, the Evoy women struggled to steady their nerves and help calm the children, who must have asked about the whereabouts of their father and complained of hunger. At night they hunkered down in their wagons, praying for the safe passage of night into dawn. The occasional sound of gunfire jolted them from their sleep as jittery men on night watch reacted to noises heard from just beyond the flickering light of their campfires.

During the daytime marches, the crack of gunshots echoing off the adjacent ridges ratcheted up their anxiety. They could not know if the emigrants fending off Indians or merely taking shots at game. The adults were increasingly concerned about the shaky disposition of the members. Unbeknownst to the Evoy/McCourtney group, as they were departing the Pit River Valley, John Peoples was entering the valley in the opposite direction through an alternate trail cutoff. Therefore, the two trains never crossed paths at this critical moment.[2]

As Bridget's party entered the intermountain region that spanned the southern Cascades and northern Sierras, they were pushing hard to put as much distance as possible between themselves and the Hewise men. But how far would be far enough? At the time they could not know of the dangerous skirmishes going on just up trail from their column. They also could not know they were leaving the range of the Hewise and entering the territory of both the Yana and the Mountain Maidu (or "Meadow People"), who had not shown a propensity for raiding the emigrants and may have preferred to avoid them altogether.[3] Meanwhile Peoples's teamsters set up a base camp in the Pit River Valley, doubly determined to get the last of the emigrants and their livestock out of the range of the Indians. At night, People's men anxiously scanned the horizon for the inevitable signal fires flickering on the ridgetops bordering the valley. He noted, "The night of the

[October] 21st the Indians made several attempts to drive off our stock, but we were too strong and vigilant for them."[4]

As a winter storm front gathered on the horizon, the Hewise efforts to acquire beef on the hoof while it was still within easy reach were becoming increasingly bold. Early on the morning of October 26, Peoples described a particularly unnerving experience "a group of Indians charged our camp, and although fired upon by our sentinels, succeeded in getting off my whole stock of beef cattle."[5] It was at this time that the last large group of travelers, including General John Wilson's train, arrived at the government camp in the Pit River Valley and were told the gravity of their situation.[6] As if on cue, that very evening Peoples recounted, "at 12 o'clock at night, the Indian [signal] fires blazed up simultaneously from every elevated point." Believing that the Indians were preparing to make "a grand and last effort to drive off our stock and that of the emigrants," Peoples ordered several men to approach and flank the Hewise men at the nearest fire for a punishing assault meant to deliver a message—a price will be exacted for further raiding. Peoples noted, "Several Indians were killed and many injured by rife fire." The fires were immediately extinguished, and the Indians retreated. He added, "and soon all the hills were wrapt in a mantle of darkness." "The next morning there were no Indians in sight which was extremely unusual . . . they had temporarily retreated but were expected to return."[7] While Peoples's company was engaging the Native men, Bridget's group was just a few days down trail, now traveling with the family of John K. Root, formerly of the Wolverine Rangers.[8] On October 28, Bridget and her daughters encountered John McCourtney, packing up trail in search of the family train.[9] After an emotional reunion, they quickly turned their attention to the grim business confronting them— survival. McCourtney surmised that the government relief party and the family train had failed to cross paths and the family had lost the opportunity for desperately needed relief.

Deeply concerned and exasperated, on October 28, John K. Root wrote a note to the government men camped at East Spring, on the Feather River, located three or four days' travel (thirty-five miles) down trail. His letter, carried forward to the government encampment at East Spring by a packer, stated: "Your advance relief company were under a special promise to Mr. McCourtny [sic] (who had left his family a packing) to supply this company, and more especially his family, which they failed to do by taking one road and we another on Pitt's River, and they are now some one hundred miles back of us, and can do us no good."[10]

They were nearly out of provisions, their mules failing, and not knowing the range of the Hewise, they could only assume the Native men could be tracking them and probing for opportunities to raid livestock. The occasional crack of gunfire in the distance stirred the imagination. As Peoples and his assistants departed the south end of the Pit River Valley with the last of the emigrants in tow, Bridget's group was apparently well out of range on a parallel trail and unaware of the relief party. The family group would have to forge ahead on their own. Emigrants' journal entries covering this segment of the trail repeatedly mention seeing tracks of wolves and grizzlies along the trail. This was the first point on the journey where the Evoys and McCourtneys would have come into close range of dangerous predators, a new cause for anxiety. At camp the weakened and dying livestock and the travelers' food stores attracted the marauding beasts, bringing them close to the travelers' sleeping places. The sounds of rustling brush and occasional cries from livestock must have greatly frightened the families huddled in their tents. Wrapped in their buffalo robes and woolen bedrolls, they fended off their anxiety and the biting winter chill.

While Bridget's group and the relief train of John Peoples put increasing distance between themselves and the Hewise, a new threat came into focus: Icy winds began driving a weather front into the mountains, and dark clouds quickly swept through the region. The storm door had finally opened, its brisk gales blowing around Lassen Peak and the surrounding terrain with a vengeance. On October 30 and 31, heavy snowfall engulfed the mountains, prompting deep concern among government relief party and panic among the emigrants. Peoples wrote, "During the day of the 31st, the snow continued to fall, and at times with such fury, as almost to blind us, and for fear of a heavy storm I kept the men and provisions in rear of the family wagons. The road getting heavy towards noon, I was forced to stop."[11] This would be the first of a series of snowstorms to rake the Modoc/Sierra borderland over the next several days. Yet, despite the tenuous prospect for survival in this wilderness, glimpses of the human spirit emerged. J. Goldsborough Bruff, writing in his journal on the 27th, noted a scene near his camp that must have appeared surreal:

> A lively scene here at night; crowded with wagons and animals, and busy throngs of every age and sex, around their bright camp-fires. The glare of the fires on all,—tents, wagons, & cc, and tall pines, made one of the prettiest night-scenes I ever beheld. . . . People singing, laughing, whistling, & some quarreling. Around us dense forests, deep black glens, and dark mountains, and now and then the howl of a wolf pack was borne by the glen by the night breeze.[12]

But stolen moments of respite and family connection were not unique to the emigrants. Neither was turning to traditions for comfort and familiarity. As winter descended on the mountains, the Native peoples of the area, the Hewise, Mountain Maidu, and Yana also sheltered with their families in their thatched or earthen winter lodges (Astsuy) and sought solace through relationships and their oral traditions. Elders gathered with their bands in large communal lodges and shared stories, engaged in games, and perhaps danced. One historian writing about the Yana, a people living in Mill Creek Canyon just to the north of Bruff's encampment, noted, "Winter was also a time for retelling the old history of the beginning of the world and of how animals and men were made, the time to hear over again of the adventures of Coyote and Fox and Pine Martin, and the tale of Bear and Dear."[13]

These creation stories relate how Coyote, and Silver (Silver-Gray) Fox created people, plants, and animals from the primordial sea.[14] Their complex language was described by one researcher as "a curious singsong of alternating high and low tones, of long and short syllables."[15]

As the emigrants struggled through the Sierran winterscape, a new reality emerged for the group: get out of the mountains or perish! What livestock had not already succumbed to the elements soon met their end as the nighttime temperatures dipped into the twenties or below. Bridget's party was realizing that travel by wagon would soon come to an end and, with it, the means of transporting the majority of their supplies. Once that happened, they would either have to shelter in place in the wagons or advance through the snowdrifts on foot. At night, as the windblown snow enveloped their tents and wagons, they couldn't know if the snow would snuff out their lives by morning, the heavy flurries being the last sight they would ever see. As the evening hours passed, the wind and the wolves howled. Bridget, Ellen, and Margaret would have kept their anxiety in check and comforted the children more than ever. Somewhere along this section of trail, the last of their oxen perished, and they were forced to abandon their last wagon. Their mules, too, were failing and could no longer carry any weight. Ellen's daughter Jane later recalled, "Finally, it was impossible to carry all their belongings—they were told to take only what they could carry themselves. Not wanting to leave their prized dresses Mother [Ellen] and Aunt Margaret McCourtney decided to wear all their best dresses—My aunt even put on her wedding dress—Mother put on four of her best dresses and trudged along on their journey."[16] The donning of multiple dresses was also helpful in fending off the cold. Bridget also considered what she could carry on her back and the absurdity of carrying heavy coinage. Jane recounted, "Grandmother [Bridget] found carrying money was too much of a burden—she offered some to one of the men—but he said, 'No Madam I have all I can carry.' With that she just threw a pile of it on the ground." Dressed "to the nines" and liberated

Emigrants struggling through thigh-high snow drifts in the Sierras, as Bridget's company did in the final two weeks of their journey on Lassen's Cutoff. *Hutchings Illustrated California Magazine*, 1859.

of most of their belongings, the Evoy women steeled their nerves and made the final push to get out of the mountains. In this deadly winter wonderland, the frail and timid "weaker sex" of the Victorian conception was nowhere in evidence.

The snow flurries that began on October 30 continued unabated for days. On November 2, Peoples's train reached the northern edge of the Feather River Valley. As the wind-driven snow swept the Sierras that evening, Joseph Bruff, hunkered down in his tent just a few miles to the west, focused his thoughts on the suffering of the emigrants, "It roars like the angry surges on a stormy coast. Alas for the sick & helpless, in these hills tonight."[17] On the morning

of November 4 the government relief team departed the Feather
River Valley. That day, at the south end of the Feather River Valley, Peoples, leading emigrants down the main trail, encountered
three additional families who were attempting an icy river crossing. It is believed this was the small train of the Evoy, McCourtney,
and Root families. With this chance encounter, Peoples was certain he had gathered the last of the emigrant families attempting the mountain crossing. He and his men assisted most of the
women and children onto mules and placed the invalid travelers
in the remaining wagons for the last trek out of the snowbelt.[18]

After hours of breaking trail through thigh-high snowdrifts
and crossing icy creeks, they halted just west of Butte Creek, thor-
oughly spent and unable to move forward. Pinned down by snow
flurries, they hunkered down and awaited a break in the storm.
Encamped just to the west, William Swain watched families struggling through the storm as they passed his camp. His journal entry
offered a glimpse of the unfolding situation for the families:

> Here might be seen a mother wading through the snow
> and in her arms an infant child closely and thickly wrapped
> with whatever would secure it from the storm, while the
> father was close at hand exerting to the utmost in getting
> along his team, wagon and provisions,—the last and only
> hope of securing the life of the family. There might be
> seen a mother, a sister or a wife, winding along the moun-
> tain road, packing blankets and other articles, followed by
> children of every age, each with some article on his back
> or in his hands.[19]

The snow continued all night on the evening of November 4
and well into the next day. Swain noted the terrific toll taken on
the remaining stock: "daylight dawned on the lifeless carcasses
of sixteen of our oxen. . . . fallen by the blasts of the merciless
storm."[20] Some starving emigrants were able to acquire meat
by following the bloody bear and wolf tracks that led from one

excavated carcass cache to another along the snowy trail. Swain wrote, "During the whole afternoon our party waded through two feet of snow with no path, alternately leading an hour each, guided by the blazes on the trees by the sides of the road, while the fresh tracks of the Grizzley bear plainly told the story of the mountain natives."[21] With "utmost difficulty," the government teamsters and the families pushed and pulled the wagons through deep, freezing mud ("up to the boot tops") and icy creek crossings as they traversed Deer Creek Valley and eventually ascended a steep hill, where they made camp. Rebecca Reeve, traveling with the same large group as Bridget, noted: "We were travelling through snows two and a half feet in depth with a narrow pathway. It was snowing fearfully,—How anxiously we journeyed on."[22] Somewhere along the trail Ellen had lost one of her shoes and now risked frostbite. They were now traveling on a steep-sided dividing ridge, a prominent feature given the telling name of the "Devil's Backbone," separating the canyons drained by Deer Creek and Mill Creek. One portion of the ridge, referred to by Bruff and subsequent authors as "The Narrows," was barely wide enough for wagons to pass in single file.[23]

That night (November 5–6) more mules froze to death, and in the morning, Peoples conceded it was time to abandon the last of the wagons. Peoples ordered "every mule that could stand up to be saddled, and then called upon such women as could ride to mount and start ahead at once." Some travelers were too weak to ride on mules, and so were left at this camp along with some provisions and a few wagons so that they could sleep off the ground. Peoples ordered a few of his men to remain and assist in maintaining campfires and caring for the emigrants until reinforcements could be brought in from the valley to help evacuate them out of the snowbelt. Exhausted, freezing and lacking sufficient mules to carry everyone, the Evoy/McCourtney group remained at this camp "near Deer Creek" temporarily.[24] Wrapped in their buffalo robes in the abandoned wagons, the family fended off the bracing wind and snow flurries, while large fires set by a few of Peoples's teamsters provided some relief and restored sensation back to frozen feet and hands. However, sporadic heavy snowfall continued on November 6 and 7. The family concluded that rather than awaiting the return of Peoples's men with additional draft animals, they would be better off moving forward through the storm, come what may. They forged ahead, the children on muleback and the adults on foot.

Peoples and Captain Todd arrived at Davis's Ranch on November 9, where they spent the next few days acquiring foodstuffs and fresh mules. On November 12 Captain Todd returned to the mountains in a last effort to get the remaining emigrants out of the snow. Among other duties Elisha Todd was instructed by Peoples to supply the McCourtney family with two mules to help get them out of the mountains.[25] They were however unaware that the family group had reentered the trail to make the last push to the valley (Davis's Ranch or Lassen's Ranch). All the while, stragglers continued to pass by J. Goldsborough Bruff's camp near The Narrows. His journal entry for November 12 offers a possible sighting of the Evoy/McCourtney group, "Late in the afternoon some families came up, 2 packed mules, and another with paniers of carpeting [saddlebags] on each side, from which protruded the chubby faces of two small children. Father led, and the mother and others followed.—I offered them a wagon to sleep in, but they went off some distance, and built a fire and camped out."[26] Recall that Ellen had relayed to her daughter that "Two of Mrs. McCourtney's children were quite small and were placed in saddle bags on either side of one of the mules. The mule was guided by Ellen's' youngest brother James Evoy." The children were three-year-old James Francis and four-year-old Mary Ann McCourtney.

Arriving at the ranch of Colonel Peter J. Davis (Davis's Ranch) sometime in the third week of November, the Evoy/McCourtney group was among the last few hundred emigrants out of the estimated seven to nine thousand people who attempted Lassen's Cutoff in that year.[27] Stationed at Davis Ranch on November 26, Major Rucker witnessed the stragglers' deliverance from their ordeal. He wrote, "A more pitiful sight I had never before beheld. There were cripples, from scurvy, and other diseases; women prostrated by weakness, and children who could not move a limb. In advance of the wagons were men mounted on mules, who had to be lifted from their animals, so entirely disabled that they become from scurvy."[28] The Evoys' journey to the California Territory had consumed six months of their lives and—if not for their willful persistence, tenacity, and some degree of luck—it could easily have been the closing six months of their lives. The migration had been a true test of their mettle.

CHAPTER 5

Pulling the Threads of Opportunity

Men plunged wildly into every mode of dissipation to drown the homesickness so often gnawing at their hearts. They sang, danced, drank and caroused all night, and worked all day. They were possessed of the demon of recklessness.

Luzena Stanley Wilson

Temporarily thwarted from reaching the northern goldfields by the unusually robust winter weather that greeted them, the recent arrivals in the Sacramento Valley had little choice but to wait it out and recover from the toll exacted by the mountain crossing. Heavy streamflow and a quagmire of deep mud along the horse trails leading to the gold region made access difficult to impossible in many areas of the foothills, at least temporarily. Their late arrival also meant they would be largely carved out of the easier mining locations already being exploited by earlier arrivals. Adding insult to injury, the recent emigrants were becoming aware that by avoiding the traditional Sierran passes (Truckee and Carson) and opting for Lassen's Cutoff, they had added roughly 180 to 200 miles to their overland journey. Mentally and emotionally exhausted and frail, those who hunkered down in the squalor of the encampments may have pondered the stark contrast between the El Dorado of their dreams and the hard realities facing them.

After a brief period of recovery at the Davis Ranch, in early December, the Evoy/McCourtney group hit the trail again. Riding down the Sacramento Valley, the family considered their immediate future. While hundreds awaited the opening of the trails and prepared for their scramble into the gold region, the Evoy/McCourtney group, under Bridget's leadership, made their initial movements based on a shrewd assessment of the opportunities that presented themselves or that could be cultivated over time. The matriarch's nearly two decades of experience in the frontier gateway hub of St. Louis had revealed the nature of economics in an area subject to the ebb and flow of a transient population of traders, explorers, and trappers. Instead of fur trappers and explorers, California was being filled with prospectors whose needs would be narrowly defined and immediate. Penniless and motivated by hunger, many emigrants followed the impulse to acquire gold, and quickly.

The Evoys and McCourtneys had arrived in California with limited funds remaining from their liquidation of assets in St. Louis and needed to make the most of them. It was perhaps during their brief recovery at Davis's Ranch that the family learned of a new settlement situated just south of the confluence of the Feather and Yuba Rivers adjacent to a large tract known colloquially as Nye's Ranch. Here the muddy waters of the Yuba River mingle with the translucent current of the Feather River.[1] This settlement represented a uniquely strategic jumping-off place for access to the Sierran foothills just to the east and the more northerly mining settlements in the Klamath Region. The location provided a viable riverine port where small sternwheel steamships, scow schooners, and barges originating at San Francisco and Sacramento could make passage up the Feather River and unload cargo and passengers at the settlement. As such, this "gateway to the northern mines" may have reminded the Evoys and McCourtneys of their former home on the Mississippi River. The family concluded that these sister settlements were a promising and pragmatic place to gain a foothold in the economic landscape. This gateway was destined to grow rapidly and, accordingly, business enterprises could be developed in the fields of merchandising, services, and transportation. The family followed the established horse trail, or "Emigrant Road," to the Feather River encampment in December 1849 as part of the initial influx of settlers to reach the area.[2] Still relatively unspoiled, the nascent river port had a charm characteristic of the northern Sacramento Valley. As viewed from the deck of a scow schooner calling port at the settlement, Mrs. Dolly B. Bates described it thus, "The banks of the Yuba, at its junction with Feather River, are romantic in the extreme. The beautiful weeping-willows fringing the margin, the creeping vines twining their tendrils around the trunks of the trees, and the variety of shrubbery, give it a decidedly tenebrious appearance."[3]

The streamside settlements were quickly populated with miners arriving by steamer, on horseback, or on foot. On arrival they filled the riverside terraces, pitched tents, constructed crude shelters, and began seeking mining supplies. Afflicted with gold fever, the hordes of miners were intent on beating a path to the goldfields to "make their pile" as soon as conditions would allow. On the heels of the arriving miners, these sister settlements were quickly filling up with merchants, tradesmen, and other settlers.

Bridget and Ellen initially chose the Yuba settlement on the west bank of the Feather River for a home. Yuba (or Yubum as the Maidu called it) was a former rancheria of the Southern Maidu (or Nisenan) Indians who, by the summer of 1849 had been displaced and relocated to other areas within the valley and foothill region. In July 1849 David A. Cheever and Tallman Rolfe, who had purchased much of the land from Captain John A. Sutter, platted a town and subsequently advertised lots for sale. In August of that year Rolfe established a crude trading post and, at least through November and December 1849, he and Cheever were the sole occupants of the new settlement, until the first settlers arrived. The ubiquitous Gold Rush businessman Samuel Brannan and his partner George Pierson were also associated with the settlement.

On the opposite side of the Feather River from Yuba lay Nye's Ranch. The rancho's owners, Charles Covillaud and business partners, concluded that their primitive settlement needed formal organization. In accordance with the Spanish and Mexican administrative structure established by the Californios in Alta California, an alcalde form of town government was established. On January 18, 1850, a meeting was called, votes cast, and Stephen J. Field elected as alcalde of the district, a judicial officer under the Spanish and Mexican laws. Field would later emerge as a highly influential attorney and politician in the formative years of Anglo California.[4] Several names were suggested for the settlement, including "Yubafield," "Yubuville," and perhaps most compellingly "Circumdoro," apparently Spanish slang for "surrounded with gold." The name Marysville, after Mary Covillaud, the wife of Charles Covillaud, was finally settled on. As Stephen Field noted, "No sooner had he [Covillaud] made the suggestion, than the meeting broke out into loud hurrahs; every hat made a circle around its owner's head, and we christened the new town Marysville.[5] Lots were advertised for sale in the *Sacramento Placer Times*.[6]

Because most of the emigrants arriving in the valley had been forced to abandon much of their belongings, they needed to acquire the basic accoutrements for mining; namely, picks, shovels, and of course, the essential tool for placer mining, the gold pan. Bridget and Ellen quickly moved to implement the first stage of their strategy, perhaps best conveyed by the Gaelic proverb *Is fhearr lán an dùirn de cheaird na lán an dùirn de dh-òr* (A handful of trade is better than a handful of gold). But Mark Twain's pithy observation struck at the heart of the situation: "When everyone is looking for gold, it is a good time to be in the pick and shovel business,"[7] Almost immediately, the Evoy women commenced a multipronged campaign to carve out their place within the economic landscape. Never intimidated by her status or sex, Bridget typically sought out and dealt directly with the movers and shakers of the northern mining region. On her initiative her daughters followed suit. In a rare move for a single female, on February 3, 1850, twenty-one-year-old Ellen B. Evoy arrived at the land office in the Yuba settlement and made one of the very first land transactions in the settlement, buying property directly from Tallman Rolfe.[8] This would be the first of many property transactions that the Evoy women would make in and around the Yuba City–Marysville gateway region.

Ellen and Bridget commissioned the construction of a trading post of the lodgepole-and-canvas variety and entered the marketplace as independent female merchants (that is, "sole traders"). They acquired merchandise (tools, and so on) through middlemen like John Sutter and others who arranged for the shipment of supplies by boat and sold them to merchants at the Marysville waterfront. These merchants, like Bridget, Ellen, and Margaret, then offered the goods for resale to the public at a markup. The miners' fixation on getting a foothold in the nearest gulch or stream course and reaping the golden harvest before their trail mates could created a captive audience for business in the gateway. And, although the costs for equipment were immoderate, there was little appetite for haggling, and sales were brisk. To make their trading post livable, Bridget and Ellen had built a pole-and-canvas-walled addition for sleeping quarters. Little better than a tent, this cabin was hardly suitable for winter weather, especially in the low-lying northern Sacramento Valley, where the cold, dank air settled in the winter months. A wood-burning stove served as both a device to cook on and a source of heat in the drafty, calico-walled structure. These living conditions were a far cry from the family's previous homestead in St. Louis, although hardly more primitive than the earthen-floored and thatched-roof home of Bridget's youth in the hamlet of Rosegarland.

Bridget and Ellen's trading post quickly generated gold, which they reinvested in purchases of merchandise or additional properties. They added square footage to their trading post and rented out cots to boarders, a common practice in the gold region.[9] In an effort to strike while the iron was hot, in March, June, and

July 1850, Bridget purchased three additional lots within the commercial district of Yuba City from the town's founders, Rolfe and Cheever, on the strength of income generated by the Evoy trading post.[10] The lot purchased in July was directly adjacent to the general store of Rolfe and Cheever. Bridget offered these lots for rent or lease to prospective merchants. The spring and summer of 1850 saw a small but burgeoning commercial center gaining a foothold within the encampment. In April 1850, a correspondent for the *Placer Times* noted, "Yuba City is rapidly increasing. Several new stores have gone up within two weeks, and are already well stocked, and are enjoying an active trade."[11] Simultaneously, in August 1850 Bridget purchased a parcel from Peter J. Davis (of the Davis Ranch at the Lassen trailhead) in the settlement of Santa Clara adjacent to Mission Santa Clara de Asís for $400.[12] This purchase made her a pioneering Euro-American landowner, and presumably the only female one, within the settlement of Santa Clara two years prior to its establishment as a town. She also acquired and then quickly resold a parcel in the Yuba District (future Yuba County) to her son-in-law John McCourtney. The full scope of Bridget's land purchases in the crucial opening months of the Gold Rush in 1850 are unknown, but at a minimum they equaled at least $32,614 in 2024 dollars.[13] The growth of the local real property market was robust. Stephen J. Field, for example, saw a tenfold increase in the value of his Marysville lots within the first ninety days of 1850. With the emergence of the northern mining region as one of the most productive gold mining regions in the American West, economic opportunity within this gateway community made a brisk ascent. By the end of 1850, Marysville and Sacramento had become the primary urban centers serving the northern mining region.[14] Within a few years Marysville would become the third largest city in California, at least for the interim.

In this initial phase of the Gold Rush, miners were too preoccupied with the pursuit of gold to produce goods, and hence the transitory population relied on imports for almost everything they needed. The void was filled by merchants from around the world

VIEW OF THE PLAZA MARYSVILLE ALT. CALIF.
Published by Cooke & LeCount Montgomery St. S.F.

Riverbank scene, Marysville, California, circa 1851. Courtesy of the California Lettersheet Collection, Kemble Special Collection 09, California Historical Society.

anticipating payment in gold. A service economy sprang up nearly overnight to meet the needs of the miners, from food, clothing, and shelter to entertainment and all the other expenditures of daily life. Despite the widespread and frenzied economic activity, the rarity of currency in the territory presented a challenge for commerce. The miners did not produce gold coinage, they produced the raw material for currency: nuggets or, more commonly, flakes of fine gold mixed with sand and silt; that is, gold dust. Gold dust represented value that the miners could exchange for supplies and luxuries. They might also send some dust home to their families in distant lands. But gold dust was not currency. The defining economic problem of Gold Rush California was to find the financial means to convert gold dust into money.[15] Within the mining camps transactions were handled rather informally through the concept of the "pinch." The customer would place a small quantity of dust on the counter and the merchant would take as much as they could pick up between thumb and forefinger (that is, a pinch). Accordingly, handheld apothecary scales were the ubiquitous tool of the trade for Gold Rush merchants such as the Evoys and McCourtneys.

Meanwhile, Margaret and John McCourtney ventured outside of Marysville in search of a suitable location to establish a base of sorts, ideally at a strategic location suitable for capturing commerce. This led them to the foothills just east of Marysville, an area that, in the late fall of 1849, was the locus of a rich discovery of placer gold within the watersheds of Wolf Creek and Deer Creek in future Nevada County. Miners flocked into the foothills and exploited the placers along the streams and dry gulches.[16] Within a few months, the bustling settlements of Nevada, Grass Valley, and Rough and Ready materialized. The settlements filled out in a chaotic maze of tents and crude lean-to hovels within the drainages of Deer Creek, Wolf Creek, and Bear River. Populated with young men caught up in the cycle of boom and bust, the transient camps were viewed by the McCourtneys as an unsuitable place for raising their young family. They got wind of an established horse trail leading from Sutter's Fort through Johnson's Ranch and across the Bear River, which on a seasonal basis provided one of the few access routes to these new mining settlements in the adjacent foothills. But the trail was prone to closure when the Bear River flowed hard. Anticipating this as a natural thoroughfare to the emergent mining stronghold, Margaret and John bought a large parcel where the horse trail forded the river. They erected a canvas-and-pole home and in the fall of 1850, John McCourtney joined with a new business partner, Alexander Van Court, in financing the construction of a toll bridge across the river.[17] This bridge provided a reliable stream crossing and in short order the trail became an important overland route between the Sacramento Valley and the rapidly developing mining settlements just to the northeast.[18] Nevada and Grass Valley soon emerged as some of the most productive mining districts in the California Territory.

For the newcomers, the foothill region represented a vast expanse of natural resources: gold, lumber, and water. In the American ethos of taming nature, these resources existed to be exploited for profit. Neither the Indigenous peoples nor the environmental impact of mining and logging activities were considered. The miners themselves were described variously as adventurers engaged in a just pursuit of nature's bounty or a reprehensible lot driven by greed and self-interest. As one Scottish immigrant, James Beith, commented wryly, "If the gates of hell were hinged with Gold, a Yankee would go there and take them."[19] However, Sarah Royce, living in a Sierran mining camp at the time, noted that "in almost every mining camp there was enough of the element of order, to control, or very much influence the opposite forces."[20] Dislodged from the civilized atmosphere of their former hometowns and living hand to mouth, many men in the camps adopted bad habits and often squandered what gold dust they acquired. As Luzena Wilson wrote, "Men plunged wildly into every mode of dissipation to drown the homesickness so often gnawing at their hearts. They sang, danced, drank and caroused all night, and worked all day. They were possessed of the demon of recklessness. Blood was often shed, for a continual war raged between the miners and the gamblers."[21] Indeed, to the casual observer, it might have seemed that for every ounce of gold that was liberated from the Sierran streams, an equal amount was liberated from the miners' pockets in the gambling halls, saloons, and bordellos of the settlements. The early newspaper editors admonished the inhabitants in print, offering a cynical view of the settlements and describing them as a "sea of iniquity" or, more creatively, "a vortex of penury and disgrace."[22] The fleeting nature of prospecting was driven in part by the miners' ignorance of the geologic origin of gold and the best practices for extracting it. Lack of knowledge compounded by the impatience of youth left many miners frustrated to exhaustion. As a journalist pointed out, "It was only the *rich strikes* that found their

Miners working a placer deposit circa 1851. "Alas! many of them had found a shelter in the almost inaccessible fastnesses of the mountains, remote from the regular settlements, and beyond the reach of organized vigilance committees" (Bates, *Incidents on Land and Water*, 121). Courtesy of the Meriam Library Special Collections Department, California State University–Chico.

way into the newspapers and hence the false idea entertained by most of those who came to California in the sanguine expectation of amassing sudden fortunes by gold digging."[23] For the overwhelming majority, expectations were crushed, but many chose to stay and turn their hand to some other, more pragmatic vocation.

Miners were typically far too occupied in the pursuit of panning to tend to their basic daily needs and there was a high demand in the camps for domestic services. Consequently, female emigrants arriving in California found an open marketplace.[24] In the initial phase of the rush, 1849–52 a relatively modest number of women captured a place in the local economy of the mother lode region.[25] Within the diggings, both married and single women washed and mended clothes, and cooked for the miners at crude impromptu tent lodges or over firepits. Women worked for wages, serving as barmaids in taverns or gambling halls, as teachers, as entertainers in dance halls, and even as childcare providers. Thereby, the women contributed to their own family economy by doing labor and creating goods that made cash expenditures unnecessary, or by providing goods and services that brought in family income. Some single women ended up working as prostitutes in the brothels, providing future authors with a mother lode of source material for colorful yarns filled with such euphemisms as "soiled doves," "painted ladies," or "ladies of the night." While some married women operated hotels in the larger cities of San Francisco or Sacramento (as did Sarah Royce, Margaret Frink, and Mary Jane Megquire), within the actual mining settlements some women ran primitive boarding houses including Louisa "Dame Shirley" Clapp of Rich's Bar, Charity Hayward of Sutter Creek, Dolly B. Bates of Marysville, and Abby Mansur of Horseshoe Bar.

The Nevada County census for 1850, for example, recorded that four of the thirteen women living in Grass Valley kept boarders. In adjacent Nevada City, twelve of the twenty-three female residents kept boarders or ran hotels, and an additional three women worked in family-run taverns that took in boarders.[26] In fact, by mid-1850, Luzena Stanley Wilson, Phoebe Ann Kidd, Martha Womak, and C. E. Stamps all operated boardinghouses in Nevada City. Like Bridget and Ellen, some women simply cordoned off portions of their canvas cabins for feeding miners and/or for providing sleeping quarters. Luzena Stanley Wilson, living with her husband in the gold camp of Nevada (City) opened their home to provide cooked meals for the miners, an enterprise that proved immediately successful. Wilson recalled, "When my husband came back at night he found . . . twenty miners eating at my table. Each man as he rose put a dollar in my hand and said I might count him as a permanent customer. I called my hotel 'El

Dorado.'" Dinnertime at the Wilsons', not unlike at the Evoys' tent lodge, would see miners congregating around hewn log tables and seated on tree stumps, only too happy to eat a cooked meal. The Wilsons reportedly made roughly $40,000 from their operation within the first six months of their arrival in the foot-hill settlement.[27] Luzena Wilson, like Bridget and Ellen Evoy, also occasionally provided loans to residents of the mining communities at a robust interest rate of 10 percent per month.

Despite the opportunities for enterprise in the gold region, married women were legally prohibited from acting as financial players independent of their husbands. Whereas Bridget (a widow) and her single daughter Ellen were not affected by this legal restriction, Margaret would have been constrained within the legal framework. Under nineteenth-century common law, a married woman was subject to the rules of coverture, which tied her legal rights with her husband's. A husband controlled his wife's earnings, as well as any property she acquired before and after marriage. Married women were prohibited from entering contracts without the husband's consent and technically could not engage in trade on their own account. Nevertheless, emulating her mother's business acumen, Margaret pursued her own independent business ventures with apparent facility. She would find work-arounds to these oppressive legal restrictions.

By situating themselves several miles outside the mining communities, the McCourtneys could minimize competition. By late 1850 they were developing a versatile commercial operation and soon expanded their facilities with a trading post and a blacksmith shop at what became known as McCourtney's Crossing.[28] Their establishment served the foot packer, the wagon or pack mule trains, and soon the stagecoach. In addition to buying supplies, travelers could get their horses shoed and perhaps get a wagon repaired. Here, Margaret soon established a boardinghouse, where weary travelers heading to the settlements might get a welcome respite, a warm meal, and a good night's sleep.[29] On rare occasions the crossing served as a venue for weddings. These expanded services could also serve the burgeoning merchant class, who by this time were becoming a growing segment of the local population. The McCourtneys acquired cattle and established a ranch and vegetable plots at their crossing, which allowed them to provide the family and their boarders with vegetables, meat, and dairy products.[30] As the McCourtney's Crossing enterprise grew, Margaret struggled to balance the diverse management responsibilities with her familial obligations and reached out for help. In 1850–51, Bridget and Ellen relocated to the McCourtney homestead temporarily to help run the boardinghouse and general store.[31] There was also the responsibility of running the ranch. On any given day, laborers might be engaged in cutting lumber, tilling the fields, irrigating the orchards, cultivating, repairing the facilities, and caring for the livestock. John was kept busy with milling lumber and blacksmithing. The relentless work of handling sales, attending to boarders, cooking, cleaning, fielding inquiries and negotiating with customers, collecting bridge tolls, and so on was handled by Bridget and Ellen. Although the crossing was removed from the settlements, this did not shield it from adversity. Theft, financial crime, and violence were never far away, Accusations made within the camps could quickly lead to retribution. As one woman in Marysville asserted, "No law was acknowledged except Lynch law; and the penalty for offences, so summarily enforced by the vigilance committees, served admirably to keep in check the murderous, villanous [sic] propensities of too many of the refugees from justice from all parts of the world. Alas! many of them had found a shelter in the almost inaccessible fastnesses of the mountains, remote from the regular settlements, and beyond the reach of organized vigilance committees."[32] Robberies, assaults and, on occasion, murders occurred in the isolated East Bear River Township over the first several years. The McCourtneys would be robbed at gunpoint in their place of business at least twice.

This adversity played out against simmering tensions between the newcomers and Native peoples. The gold-seeking interlopers who concentrated their mining activities in the areas east of Yuba

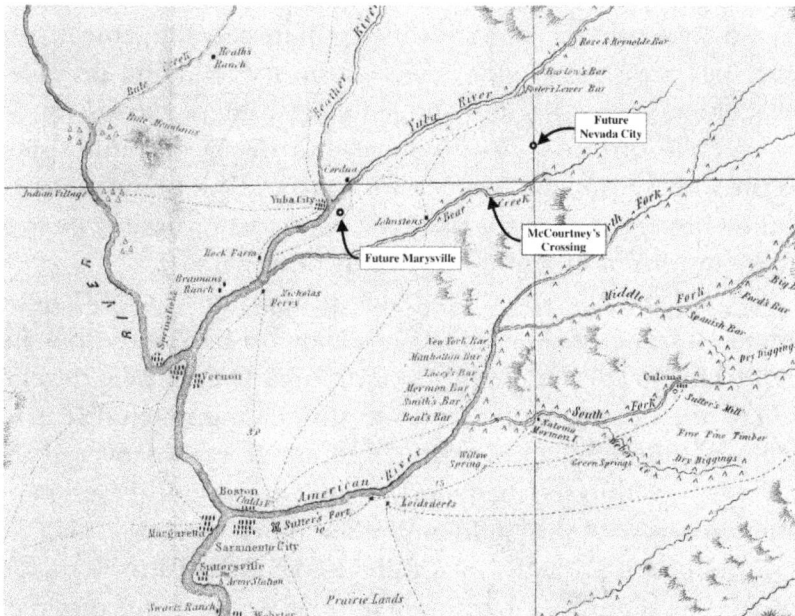

William A. Jackson's Map of the Mining District of California, December 1849. Courtesy of the David Rumsey Map Collection, David Rumsey Map Center, Stanford University Libraries.

City–Marysville occupied the traditional territory of the Southern Maidu. which spanned the American, Bear, and Yuba River watersheds. Disease, displacement, and social decline took a cumulative toll on these and other adjacent tribes. The Indigenous people were forced into the status of an impoverished minority living on the periphery of the more desirable lands of the valley and foothill regions, now under Euro-American control.[33] Rancherias in the northern Sacramento Valley consolidated so that the survivors could continue to live in communities controlled by their traditional social hierarchy.[34] One outcome of this situation was a series of violent skirmishes between elements of the emigrant population and some Indians in the northern mining region, usually triggered by the impulsive acts of a few, which sometimes led to a violent cycle of organized retribution between some miners and Natives.[35] The overwhelming superiority in numbers and weaponry gave settlers every advantage in this deadly game of attrition.[36] On occasion, cooler heads amongst the Maidu prevailed. Tribal elders stepped in and applied their influence to disrupt the vicious cycle of retributive violence. But the larger atmosphere was rife with tension and primed for conflict. This potential would soon be brought home for the Evoy/McCourtney family through a random turn of luck and in a deeply personal way.

As gold fever reached epidemic proportions in the gateway settlement, nineteen-year-old James Evoy bristled at the ties that bound him to the family business at Yuba City. A new development in the mining settlements was stimulating much discussion locally, piquing the young man's interest. It was discovered that quartz veins within the metamorphic belt in the mother lode were sometimes infused with gold and other alloyed metals. As early as 1851, public attention in Grass Valley and Nevada City was turning toward the potential of hard rock mining ("quartz reef mining"), an alternative method to the water-intensive placer mining.[37] The incessant chatter of prospectors who "kitted out" at the Evoy trading post on their way to adventure and potential reward in the mining settlements was ultimately too much to resist for James Evoy. He decided to try his luck at hard rock mining in the new settlement of Nevada, situated a dozen miles east of Marysville.[38] This decision, seemingly innocuous at first, would prove fateful. James soon obtained a job at a mining claim near Nevada. This arduous work required the occasional use of explosives to liberate the source rock from the outcrops. Recalling family oral tradition, Jane Montgomery later wrote:

> On one occasion [Bridget's] young son James was at the mine and a call was made for someone to go for blasting powder—the men were afraid to go, as the Indians had threatened to kill the first white man they saw, in reprisal for the killing of an Indian. James liked the Indians, he was not afraid—so he jumped on his horse and galloped away—but was never seen again—supposedly killed by the Indians.[39]

The ambush reportedly took place near Longs Bar, a placer mining settlement located within an area traditionally occupied by the Southern Maidu.[40] In truth, this was most likely a chance encounter where James, riding along the trail on horseback, surprised some Maidu men who perhaps saw an opportunity to avenge recent violence against their people. Within the mining camps, vigilante justice followed a familiar pattern: a sentence was issued promptly and punishment dealt out hastily within hours of the crime. Incensed at James's killing, a vigilante group quickly formed at Marysville. Heated speeches were made and anger spilled over within the ranks, leading to a rash decision that quick, violent retribution was needed to send a message to the local Maidu. In deference to the matriarch, the ad hoc committee visited Bridget at her home, offered their condolences and vowing "to kill off all the Indians of that tribe." As Jane later recalled, Bridget soundly rejected the proposal: "Grandmother said, 'No, gentlemen—that will not bring back my boy.'" Over the succeeding days, word of Bridget's stance on retribution filtered back to some of the Maidu elders. Perhaps sensing that she held some influence within the community, the Maidus made a gesture of reconciliation and gratitude for her support: "so the Indian Chief and several of his braves called on her and promised, 'There will be no more killings.'"[41] In a period of deep mourning, Bridget's thoughts turned to her only other son, John. She had not heard from him since the opening weeks of the overland migration in Missouri, well more than a year prior, and was unsure of his whereabouts or even his fate. In late January 1851, she placed a public notice in the *Marysville Herald* seeking information on John's whereabouts and offering information on how he could find her and Ellen. Her public notices extended over a month, apparently without success. John was presumably engaged in the hand-to-mouth existence of a miner in some remote camp, incommunicado either by circumstance or by choice. Several years would pass before he would emerge from the gold region apparently devoid of riches and settle in the Francisco Bay Area.

The Evoy/McCourtney family's movements within the gateway region brought them into contact with a number of movers and shakers who operated diverse financial interests between the crucial river ports of Sacramento and Yuba City–Marysville. In July 1850, John McCourtney partnered with Serranus C. Hastings to provide a mortgage loan to John S. Fowler for the partnership of Fowler & Semple to purchase a commercial lot in Sacramento City. Serranus Hastings was a prominent attorney in California who served as an early chief justice of the Territory of California (1849–51) and later as California state attorney general (1852–54).[42] He earned a small fortune through his law practice and used that fortune to finance his real estate ventures.[43] Posthumously, Hastings's legacy was tainted over his role in facilitating a violent campaign to displace Yuki Indians around his large ranch in Eden Valley, Humboldt County, in 1856–59.[44] John S. Fowler was well connected with prominent financial players of the Sacramento Valley and was a sometime partner of the ubiquitous Gold Rush entrepreneur Samuel Brannan. Additionally, he acted as an agent for John A. Sutter and, in 1849, had a virtual monopoly on shipping between Sacramento City and the settlements of the northern Sacramento Valley.[45] In late 1850 Fowler reneged on his loan, and McCourtney and Hastings brought suit against the partnership of Fowler & Semple, eventually receiving a judgment against the future "Sheriff's sale" of Fowler's downtown Sacramento commercial property.[46]

Meanwhile McCourtney's Crossing gained a higher profile for travelers. As early as 1851, a stagecoach "express line" was established on the wagon road that extended to the foothill region via the McCourtney toll bridge. Advertised extensively within the northern Sacramento Valley region, this stage service provided regular transport to and from the settlements of Nevada City, Grass Valley, and Rough and Ready, fostering growth for the fledgling communities. The crossing would continue to serve as a scheduled stage stop throughout the next few decades. The McCourtneys' business establishment benefited from the increasing volume and diversity of travelers along their route, some of whom were merchants and others intending to conduct business in the settlements but not necessarily wishing to settle there.

Meanwhile, Bridget and Ellen periodically returned to their home at Marysville to conduct business and collect rents and payments on mortgage loans they had made. The community had been filling out during Bridget's and Ellen's absences, as reflected in the census records. Most of their neighbors were identified as farmers, traders, laborers, and seasonal miners.[47] Nevada City and Grass Valley were also evolving into more permanent settlements, which led to the construction of sturdier wood-frame structures in lieu of the previous, crude pole-and-canvas dwellings. In order to tap this new marketplace for milled lumber, in 1851 John constructed a sawmill and began harvesting timber from his foothill acreage.

Prospectors working the placer deposits in the summer and fall seasons soon learned that access to a reliable water source facilitated the washing and mechanical separation of placer gold from the sediments excavated from the creek banks, streamside terraces, and dry gulches.[48] As the easily accessed deposits along active watercourses began to diminish by 1851, miners began to divert water toward placer sediments located farther afield through the construction of earthen ditches or wooden flumes. Through this process, placers could be washed in long toms, wood cradles, or sluice boxes.[49] This practice caused significant erosion and quickly generated massive quantities of sediment (tailings), which were carried by runoff and deposited downstream during and following storms. This manipulation of runoff patterns had a significant environmental impact and produced a cascading effect on fluvial ecosystems throughout the foothill and valley regions.[50] Simultaneous with this, and in response to the depletion of placer diggings at the ground surface, a new mining process was developed, referred to colloquially as "coyoteing."

This process entailed digging a vertical shaft through the streamside alluvium down to the underlying bedrock, which in some locations was infused with quartz veins. The bedrock was hand-excavated and the rubble raised to the ground surface by a windlass system powered by a horse, donkey, or mule. A horse-driven windlass was, by definition, rated at one horsepower.[51] Miners working within the confines of small tunnels crawled on their hands and knees to excavate and remove the spoils. This was unhealthy and dangerous work, especially when combined with subsurface water flows that could destabilize the confining tunnels. The resulting small sinkholes and vertical shafts across the ground surface resembled coyote dens, which gave this type of mining the name coyoteing. By late 1850, merchants had become major investors in the coyote operations and the water ditch construction that sustained and promoted mining in the area.[52]

In the summer and fall of 1851, John McCourtney began exploiting this mining method at a promising location called Wet Hill, just northeast of the settlement of Nevada.[53] The immediately surrounding area was called the "Coyote Lead" or, in miners' parlance, "Cayote Lead." For this venture, McCourtney partnered with a man with the surname Myers, their claim referred to as "McCourtney and Myers' Shaft." An article describing the mining venture in the early fall of 1851 described the claim as follows:

> The depth of the lead, the sandy nature of the earth, and the great amount of water in the hill [infiltration of winter rains filling the workings] compels the use of horse power instead of the common hand windlass—some four or five horse shafts are being worked on the hill, and the results from the working is such as warrant the heavy expense. A specimen of pipe clay was shown to us a day or two since from McCourtney & Myers' shaft, which was literally stuffed with gold, the Oro peeping out on every side of the mass. In the claims worked by the above gentlemen, $49 to the pan has been found. In the claims of Livers, Kline & Co,, nearby, as high as $93 to the pan: has been found. It is no uncommon thing to take pans of $12, $13, and $20 from claims on this hill.[54]

With the competent team of Margaret, Ellen, and Bridget maintaining the McCourtney's Crossing enterprises, John had the luxury of developing the Coyote Lead claim at Nevada for extended periods. His daily takes of gold held a value up to thirty-three times the daily wages he had earned as a ship's carpenter at St. Louis. Like most individual efforts, John's mining venture probably lasted a season or two before his claim was exhausted. Within a few years of Wet Hill's initial operations, McCourtney's partner Myers joined a consortium of prospectors in establishing the Myers Ravine Mining District, which reportedly became quite successful at selling claims rather than engaging in mining directly.[55]

More than any other California gold mining settlement, Nevada City and Grass Valley thrived during the first half of the 1850s primarily because their gold-bearing gravels and auriferous quartz veins were rich enough to pay despite speculative greed, ignorance of mining techniques, the unpredictable nature of the water supply and the unpredictable mountain weather of the Sierra Nevada. Once extensive gold discoveries held a promise of reasonable permanence for the towns, newspaper editors and town boosters began to argue that the highly transient society of the Gold Rush threatened organized business and mine production. These settlements lacked traditional sources of social stability and, the boosters argued, the characteristics and attitudes of Gold Rush society were detrimental. Influential residents in Nevada County, such newspaper editor Alonzo Delano, began advocating for the need to attract more women to the mining settlements to bring a civilizing effect upon these male-dominated communities. Accordingly, within just a few years, the female population of the Nevada County mining region began to rise rapidly. Simultaneous with these developments, married women's property rights acts passed in April 1852 enlarged the ability of married women to own and control separate property. These acts allowed married women to engage in trade, write contracts or engage in businesses on their own account (sole trader laws), and to keep the earnings from their labor (earnings laws).[56] Relatively rare in the first year or two of the Gold Rush, independent (married) businesswomen increased quickly along with the population of women within the mining region. From this point onward, Margaret, already prolific in her business movements, assumed sole ownership of her properties and businesses, and could enter litigation in her own name. She would thereafter be identified in public records and publications of the period as "M. P. McCourtney," entrepreneur, major landowner and boss.[57]

Along with these demographic and social changes, efforts were made to organize community governments. Local elections were held and the winners were primarily businesspeople. To gain influence in the transportation infrastructure of the community, John McCourtney ran for supervisor of roads in the Rough and Ready Township of Nevada County, and was elected to the position in 1852 and again in 1853. His appointment facilitated the ongoing maintenance of the important thoroughfare to and through the mining region and therefore the success of his toll bridge. The route was soon given the name McCourtney Road, which extended from the area of McCourtney's Crossing through to Nevada City, a distance of about thirty miles. It remains an important thoroughfare in the Nevada County to this day.

In a remarkably short time after their arrival in the territory, the Evoys and McCourtneys had managed to launch diverse entrepreneurial enterprises on multiple fronts that tapped nearly every obvious avenue of financial opportunity in the Gold Rush economy of Northern California. That this family economic unit was largely driven by the persistent efforts of its female members was particularly impressive. They had indeed struck gold, but they would have to exercise prescience and versatility in reacting to the rapidly shifting fields of opportunity in the California Territory.

CHAPTER 6

A Picturesque Character

In our rambles we often spoke of California, the beauty
of its scenery, the salubrity of its climate, the field which it
presented for enterprise, the probabilities of it becoming
a part of the United States, and the possibility of our making it the place of our future home.

Zach Montgomery

Although they couldn't know it at the time, Bridget and her family
would soon welcome a new member who would have a tremendous impact on their future: Zach Montgomery. Zach hailed from
a long line of Catholic families who emigrated from the Chesa-
peake Bay region of Maryland and settled in Kentucky between the
1790s and the 1810s.[1] Born in 1825 near Bardstown, Kentucky, Zach
would eventually become a central figure in the Evoy/McCourt-
ney extended family. His father, Thomas Francis Montgomery,
was a tobacco and sugar beet farmer. Several family members of
Thomas's and his father's generation became prominent members of the Catholic faith and clergy and were instrumental in
establishing the Catholic missions within central Kentucky.[2]

While in secondary school at Knottsville, Kentucky, in 1843,
Zach Montgomery chanced upon a book owned by his friend
Thomas Bidwell that would ultimately change the course of his
life. The book was an account of Thomas's brother John Bidwell's
journey in 1841 across the plains to the Mexican province of
Alta California.[3] Zach later wrote, "It was by reading this journal

of young John Bidwell that the mind and heart of this narra-
tor first became fascinated with California."[4] Zach and Thomas
Bidwell became roommates and fast friends at St. Mary's College
in Lebanon, Kentucky. Zach recalled, "Most of our hours of recreation were spent in each other's company, and in our rambles we
often spoke of California, the beauty of its scenery, the salubrity of
its climate, the field which it presented for enterprise, the probabilities of it becoming a part of the United States, and the possibility of our making it the place of our future home."[5]

In 1848 Zach completed his master's degree in law and soon
thereafter began practicing legal arguments in the moot court
of Judge Grigsby in Bardstown. Later that year, news of gold in
California reached Kentucky, causing a great deal of public interest and speculation through the winter of 1848–49. At the time
when Bridget and her family were making their perilous winter
mountain crossing in California (November 1849), Zach was just
beginning to grapple with the temptation posed by the sensational news from California. The news further piqued his long-
held fascination with the distant outpost of the American West. In
an invited speech at St. Joseph's College during this period, Zach
acknowledged the temptations presented by the gold discovery.
He invited his academic audience, "You too are miners, come to
dig for gold." To reconcile the motivations of greed against the
higher values held by civilized society, he added, "Not indeed that
base and drossy metal which is the miser's God; at whose shrine
fools delight to worship; you are come to dig in the gold region of
knowledge, to enrich the precious coffers of your minds, with the
precious metals of conscience."[6]

Hearing of the reported ubiquity of gold in the mountains of
California, Zach concluded the time was right for starting a new
life in the California of his earlier daydreams. In the late spring
of 1850, and with money borrowed from his father, Thomas, Zach
purchased the necessary supplies and joined a group of young
Kentuckians assembled at the jumping-off settlement of St. Joseph,
Missouri. On May 2, 1850, the group commenced their trek on

the Overland Trail.[7] His naiveté about the adversity that awaited his group was apparent when he insisted on bringing along his collection of law books in the wagon, much to the consternation of his traveling companions.[8] He envisioned practicing law after his initial take of gold. In this, he joined many professionals and tradespeople who brought the tools of their trade along on their westering journey. They had a backup plan for making a living in case the proverbial elephant eluded them, and their golden dreams were thwarted or played out after a short period. It reportedly took his train ninety days to make the Overland Trail crossing, a markedly shorter time than the trains that traveled as families. Precious little was recorded of his overland trip. In an interview with historian Alonzo Phelps many years later, Zach noted, "The journey across the plains was accomplished with its incidental trials, hardships, dangers and privations, but at last the golden goal was reached without serious mishap."[9] Zach and his company crossed the Sierra Nevada via the vaunted Carson Route and arrived safely at Sutter's Fort in Sacramento City on July 31, 1850, his law book collection apparently intact.

Taking in the unfolding scene at Sacramento, Zach described the spectacle: "The valley around the city was literally covered with tents and wagons and teams of camping parties, resting from their toilsome journey across the plains, while the roads leading to the city from the various mining localities which made Sacramento their trading point, were alive with teamsters and horsemen driving or riding at a seemingly break-neck speed. Everybody appeared to be in a hurry to 'make their pile' and get out of the country."[10] Anxious to prospect for gold, Zach departed for Ringgold, a gold-mining camp in the newly established, and aptly named, El Dorado County, a few day's horseback ride from Sacramento.[11] He and his train had passed by the general area on their way to Sutter's Fort but had continued on as they required provisions and more information on the prospects for mining locations.

Zach's fantasy that within a day or two he would be flush with gold soon burst. In writing of this experience later, he noted wryly, "One week's experience at the town of Ringgold was amply sufficient to convince the writer that *her* gold had but a feeble ring for him, and that he must try his luck somewhere else and, perhaps at some other business."[12] For his outlay of cash at the local boarding house ($16 per week) and the fee for providing pasturage for his mule ($2.50 per week) Zach was rewarded with little more than experience. He would have quickly realized that even if he had acquired placer gold, the cost of living in the gold camps was nearly equal to the average daily take of gold dust for the miner.[13] In fact geologist Philip T. Tyson, in a report to Congress in early 1850, estimated that in the first eighteen months since the discovery of gold (up through the end of 1849), the take of the average miner was about $3 per day (about $123 per day in 2024 dollars), and the high cost of living in the mining regions averaged about the same. At that rate, gold digging was less profitable than laboring back in the emigrant's home state.[14] Hence, prospectors were eternally searching for better opportunities. One writer of the period noted, "Wonderful stories are circulated in some instances to increase the population at some particular spot; and when the diggers flock to it they often find it no better than the one they left, and sometimes less productive."[15] Zach faced the conundrum every other gold prospector grappled with: "Seeing the elephant" was not unlike the experience of chasing a mirage, a reward that deftly and eternally retreated from one's grasp. Over time, though, he would come to see his adopted home in a new light, appreciating the irony of miners scrambling across the Californian landscape in an endless pursuit of the "base and drossy metal" while oblivious to the real value of this Eden on the Pacific Coast. Inspired by this observation, Zach later offered his epiphany: "California gold was a hidden treasure. But California, like a beautiful maiden—perfect in form and feature, adorned with the matchless charm of innocence, and all unconscious of her own beauty—needed not the vain glitter of gold to complete her loveliness."[16]

In this sentiment, true paradise, much like true beauty, existed in the eye of the beholder. In September 1850, California's official admittance into the Union was celebrated in Sacramento in grand style. Zach participated in the celebration. With few alternatives for long-term living arrangements in this bustling and chaotic city, he found lodging at a boardinghouse—a multiroom structure of pole-and-canvas construction with canvas walls separating adjacent sleeping quarters. But the overcrowded and chaotic state of the city was trying for the permanent residents and precipitated what was called the "Asiatic Cholera" epidemic that hit Sacramento in the winter of 1850–51. Of this Zach recalled, "For some time the plague raged with such merciless fury that almost the only active business done was the burying of the dead." He spoke eloquently of the difficult circumstances of illness and death among the "sea of strangers" in Sacramento City: "The funeral processions were indeed few and small; for, alas! those who would have moistened with tears of affection the cold clay of the dear departed, were far, far away, dreaming perhaps of the rich harvests of treasure their cherished ones were reaping upon California's fabulous fields of gold."[17] Zach's longing for open spaces, fresh air, and perhaps a new livelihood led to a decision in the winter of 1851 to take another turn at placer mining. He relocated to Hansonville, in Butte County, situated twenty-eight miles north of Marysville.[18]

After a brief stint at placer mining there, Zach concluded the easy diggings had been exhausted, so he relocated to the Churn Creek mining area in Shasta County, which according to the rumor mill, appeared promising.[19] Churn Creek had been one of the original placer-mining camps in Shasta County, extending back to 1849. Like so many others pursuing the promise of California's mineral wealth, Zach was again finding that the elusive oro remained beyond his reach. In the spring of 1852, his cabin on Churn Creek was raided by Pit River Indians and so, disheartened, he abandoned the homestead. In what may seem no small irony, the future community of Montgomery Creek (named in honor of Zach) on a tributary of the Pit River in Shasta County would later become the home of a federal Indian reservation for the Pit River peoples (the Montgomery Creek Rancheria).[20] After fruitless attempts at mining, Zach finally accepted that opportunity in the gold region was best realized through serving the community while leaving the pursuit of gold to others. In the spring of 1853, he relocated to the boomtown of Shasta City, described as "the lusty queen city of California's northern mining district."[21] Here he opened a law practice in partnership with William Daingerfield. Many of his clients were miners, farmers, and ranchers who rarely had the luxury of affording professional legal services. Accordingly, his law practice provided a very modest income and showed little, if any, potential for growth.

Although this early phase of his life in California was not auspicious, it would not be long before Zach Montgomery would embark on a remarkable ascent within the professions of law, politics, newspaper publishing, literature, and public oratory.[22] These choices reflected his interests, which were primarily intellectual. In the latter half of the nineteenth century, he would emerge as a highly accomplished and influential character in California history, someone a fellow assemblyman described as a "picturesque character." His law career reached its peak in the late 1880s, when he served as the US assistant attorney general in the first administration of President Grover Cleveland.[23] Zach and many of the people he interacted with in legal and political circles would eventually fill the history books touching on the formative period of American California. But most important for this story is his eventual connection with the Evoys and McCourtneys.

CHAPTER 7

Rodeado de Oro

Surrounded with Gold

In the early days the incentive lay greatly in the cravings
of a feverish imagination, excited by camp-fire tales of
huge ledges, and glittering nuggets, the sources of these
bare sprinkling precious metals which cost so much toil to
collect.

Hubert Howe Bancroft, 1888

In the spring of 1852, the Sierran foothills and northern Sacramento Valley were hit with a series of large-scale storms, producing massive runoff that devastated Marysville and adjacent
areas. Residential and commercial properties and ranches within
the settlement were inundated, flood damage was widespread,
and an unknown number of lives were lost. The Bear River over-
spilled its banks and washed away the toll bridge at McCourtney's
Crossing.[1] The bridge would soon be replaced, but the flooding
and associated damage threw the local economy into chaos for a
while. Bridget, Ellen, and other residents at Marysville salvaged
what was left of their homes and businesses, unaware that their
current plight was a harbinger of things to come. Back-to-back
series of floods were exacerbated by the practice of uncontrolled
timber harvesting in the foothills. Deforestation stripped away forest cover and tree root systems, dramatically increasing the volume of surface runoff and erosion within the natural watersheds

and focusing it in areas of development and infrastructure. Additionally, the practice of hydraulic mining, involving the application of large quantities of water sprayed at high velocity into the hillsides by water cannons (Monitors), added considerably to the accumulation of debris within the watersheds. The result: severe erosion and washouts in the foothills and deposition of vast sediment fields in the lowlands along river courses that drained the Sierras. Several years would pass before this problem could be addressed, primarily through the efforts of activist farmers in the Central Valley, comprising the combined Sacramento and San Joaquin Valleys.

The increasingly impactful flooding, outbreaks of cholera, and a devastating fire at Marysville, which caused an estimated $500,000 in damage, may have prompted Bridget and Ellen to begin looking to relocate farther afield. Through their growing network of contacts, they learned of the booming mining settlements along Clear Creek in Shasta County.[2] This information may have come though Major Pierson B. Reading, with whom they did business in Yuba City as early as 1850. The Clear Creek drainage had an obscure but important history in the Gold Rush. In May 1848, Major Reading and his Indian laborers discovered placer gold within the Clear Creek area. It is estimated that between 100 and 150 miners wintered there in 1849–50, mining in all the gulches (dry diggings) that ran into Clear Creek between the encampments of Briggsville and Muletown.[3] From the onset of the Gold Rush, Clear Creek and its many tributaries became the southern boundary of the most important gold mining district in the Klamath Mountain region. An encampment called Horsetown served as the headquarters of the local mining operations. From Clear Creek, miners branched out into the tributary creeks and gulches, especially during the winter when runoff could be used to wash the auriferous gravels of their detrital gold through panning, sluicing, and the use of long tom rockers. One historian noted of the Clear Creek placer diggings, "Gold was plentiful. Miners averaged from one ounce to $200 a day by the pan method."[4] While the creek channels were probably mined quite early, the alluvium forming the streamside terraces was also exploited for placer gold. Whether by ground sluicing or other forms of mechanical placer separation, exploitation of the stream terraces by running water necessitated the construction of diversions and delivery systems (ditches or flumes). As early as 1850, a road of sorts was established that extended from Red Bluff and provided access to the Clear Creek settlements of Horsetown and Briggsville, then ran northward through Shasta City.[5]

Sometime in mid-spring of 1852, Bridget secured property at Briggsville, the small mining settlement adjacent to Horsetown on the north bank of Clear Creek. By June of that year, she and Ellen had settled into the placer camp, presumably contracting a laborer to help construct a pole-and-canvas structure as they had done elsewhere. The California State Population Census of 1852 identified the vast majority of people living there as miners, whereas Bridget and Ellen were listed as merchants, a rare occupation in the Clear Creek diggings.[6] Bridget and Ellen followed their proven formula for securing a place in the local economy: supplying goods to the miners via a trading post. Once they gained a foothold, they would build on that success by expanding their commercial operation. All the while, they relied on income through mortgage payments and rents from their other properties located elsewhere, along with occasional property sales. Sometime early in the middle months of 1852, they commissioned the construction of a wood-frame structure, a boardinghouse/eatery named California House, in honor of their adopted state. The population census indicates the Evoys had a teenage Indian laborer by the name of Peter living on the premises. Bridget and her daughters had a long tradition of bringing in young orphans, and Peter may have been one. Depending on their background and strengths, these young people helped in the home, assisted with childcare, or performed ranch duties. Perhaps naively, they may have thought that they could provide the orphans with a decent home and salvation from a worse fate, an extension of their Christian sensibilities. Peter most likely helped out with maintenance chores and care of the livestock. A newspaper advertisement placed by Bridget offered a description of the Evoy establishment: "There is attached to the premises a kitchen, dining and sleeping rooms, all well-furnished, together with a corral and a quantity of hay: also, a wagon, two horses, harness, stables, three milch cows, several head of young cattle, and much other valuable property."[7] The horses and wagon were used for making trips into Shasta City for supplies, business errands, and social visits. For travel to their more distant business interests, Bridget and Ellen relied on the stage line that ran through the Clear Creek settlements. Bridget's maintaining cows at the place suggests she was able to provide such items as milk and butter to her boarders, a luxury in the mining settlements. A newspaper article published in June 1852 described Briggsville as "quite a lively little place, with a woman in it. And nearby is a rich flat of deep diggings and coyoteings."[8] Although the woman was not identified, this undoubtedly was a reference to Bridget.

The Evoy women and their counterparts running lodging houses within the mining camps were often far from the rare marketplaces such as Marysville or Rancho Chico. They were as isolated as the miners they served. Contemporaneous women wrote of the logistics of running such an enterprise. Mary Ballou, who ran a boardinghouse at a settlement called Negro Bar, provided a glimpse of the endless labor required to run such an operation in a remote mining camp. In a letter to her son Selden, she described the variety of cooked fare she prepared for the haggard miners who wandered into her canvas-and-lodgepole "house" three times a day. While they congregated at the long, hand-hewn log table, Ballou served up "soups, cranberry tarts, fried trout, roasted chicken, eggs, boiled cabbage, turnips, fried fritters, broiled steak, and potatoes."[9] Although the food was very basic, the cooking was almost nonstop. But the chance to eat home-cooked food gave the homesick miners some comfort and perhaps a sense of normalcy reminiscent of their former homes. It also provided them with a chance to catch up on local gossip and mining intelligence, the former often indistinguishable from the latter. The daily operations of the California House would have been similar to what Ballou described, a life of perpetual toil from sunup to well past sundown. But Bridget and Ellen had the added duties of caring for the farm animals, collecting eggs, milking cows, washing clothes for the miners, and making occasional runs by stage into Shasta City, a dozen miles to the north. Maintaining an organized, comfortable lodging establishment was nearly impossible in the primitive and chaotic setting with the marginal protection offered by the calico-walled pole building. Of these practical challenges Ballou related, "Anything can walk into the kitchen that choses to walk in and there being no door to shut from the kitchen into the dining room . . . sometimes I am up all night scaring the hogs and mules out of the house." Although already well occupied in running her business, Ballou occasionally dusted off a "long tom" rocker and attempted to extract "color" (gold flakes) from the placers. She stated, "I am doing a little mining in this gold region but I think it harder to rock the cradle to wash out gold than it is to rock the cradle for the Babies in the States." She also noted how well she was treated, belying the reputation of the mining camps: "Here I am among the French and Duch and Scoth and Jews and Italions and Sweeds and Chineese and Indians and all maner of tongus but I am treated with due respect by all of them." Ballou added significantly, "I would not advise any Lady to come out here and suffer the toil and fatigue that I have suffered for the sake of a little gold neither do I advise any one to come."[10] Such opinions were not exclusive to women in El Dorado. Expressing similar sentiments, miner Willian Swain wrote to his brother back home:

A man has to make a jackass of himself packing loads over mountains that God never designed man to climb, a barbarian by foregoing all the comforts of civilized life. . . . Tell all whom you know that are thinking of coming that they have to sacrifice everything and face danger in all its forms, for George, thousands have laid and will lay their bones along the routes to and in this country. Tell all that "death is in the pot" if they attempt to cross the plains and hellish mountains.[11]

In the period from mid-1852 through 1853, Ellen and Bridget were also managing their properties in Marysville, Yuba City, and Yreka which required occasional, jarring stagecoach rides to these communities. The Hall and Crandall Stage had recently established a route running between Sacramento and Yreka and, for the local segment, the stage departed Shasta City early in the morning, made a stop at Briggsville, and arrived at Marysville the following morning. Juggling all these enterprises must have been exhausting and occasionally required selling off some assets to keep Bridget's larger business interests manageable. In the late spring of 1853, she entered into a mortgage agreement with Stephen Lean, lending

ROSS'S BAR, CALIFORNIA.

This lithograph of a scene at Ross's Bar, Yuba County, shows a boardinghouse of the pole-and-canvas variety typical of the mining region. *Gleason's Pictorial Drawing-Room Companion*, 1854.

him money to purchase a portion of her parcel in Briggsville on payments. Lean, a prominent citizen, soon thereafter established the Lean Hotel in the boomtown.[12]

Having earned the equivalent of $73,791 (in 2024 dollars) in just less than one year, Bridget was "hitting paydirt" on a daily basis, not in the streams and gulches of Clear Creek but through her business enterprises in Briggsville. As of May 1853, she had accumulated $1,800 in gold dust from her boardinghouse and recent property transaction. She had seen the mythical elephant of the argonaut after all! Caches of gold dust, however, invited opportunities for robbery, so she occasionally had to remove the accumulated gold from her place of business. To do so, she would have to make the long trip by stage to Marysville to make a secured deposit at a bank, while taking advantage of the opportunity to conduct business locally and visit Margaret and John at McCourtney's Crossing several miles to the southeast. Twenty-five-year-old Ellen, by now a seasoned sole trader, had become adept at overseeing the operation of the hostelry in her absence. On May 25, 1853, only two days after she entered into her contract with Stephen Lean, Bridget boarded the stage at Briggsville with a heavy carpetbag containing the $1,800 in gold dust divided into two buckskin satchels, weighing several pounds each.[13] The stage route to Marysville included stops at the settlements of Tehama, Rancho Chico, and Nye's Ranch at the mouth of the Yuba River. Rancho Chico was John Bidwell's homestead and expansive farm, so it was most likely through these trips that Bridget became acquainted with Bidwell, another important figure in the annals of Northern California history.[14] Traveling through the remote northern mining region with a large amount of gold was fraught with risk for even the hardiest souls. Bridget was savvy enough to know to use discretion, but as woman in her sixties traveling unescorted, she would be at heightened risk. While en route she was befriended by one of the fellow passengers, Colonel John H. Harper, a prominent citizen of Butte County and a former state senator who had represented the district encompassing Trinity and Klamath Counties in 1852.[15]

Colonel Harper was attentive to Bridget during the long stage ride, perhaps winning her trust to a degree. At one point in the journey, the travelers stopped for a rare break at a stage stop called Dry Creek House, and the passengers exited the coach and went inside to get water, stretch, and make inquiries on the conditions of the route ahead.[16] Colonel Harper offered to keep an eye on Bridget's heavy carpetbag while she entered the ranch house for a break. He may have assumed this middle-aged widow, traveling alone, might be influenced by his high social standing and would be an easy mark to take advantage of. If he had made such an assumption, he would soon learn otherwise. When Bridget returned to the coach along with other passengers, she grasped her carpetbag and noticed its weight seemed different. Looking inside, she realized her gold dust satchels had been removed and replaced with rocks of a similar weight. Incredulous that this clever deception could have played out under Harper's watchful eye, Bridget immediately confronted him. As the bewildered travelers gathered around the coach, voices raised to a high pitch. Hardly a frail or timid woman, the tenacious widow tore into the colonel. Harper feigned shock at the accusation. Becoming increasingly animated and flinging his overcoat aside in a dramatic gesture, he pronounced his willingness to be searched. The coat landed on the ground with a heavy thud and another passenger (identified only by the surname Cummings), perceiving something was amiss, picked it up and pulled a satchel of gold out of the pocket. Bridget's name was marked on it. On a further search of Harper's coat, a second satchel containing upward of a thousand dollars in gold dust was found in his other pocket.[17] Harper claimed ignorance as to how the first satchel made it into his pocket but asserted that the second satchel was his own. At a later hearing before Justice Wright, Bridget explained that while she was preoccupied in the ranch house, Harper was seen by another passenger taking a stroll while, incongruously, carrying a woman's carpetbag in his hand.[18]

The local sheriff was summoned. While the other passengers were allowed to continue their trip, Colonel Harper and Bridget were transported by the sheriff to nearby Neal's Ranch, where a lengthy questioning ensued in private. A newspaper article of the period stated, "On examining the larger purse at Neal's Ranch, a piece of paper was found among the gold with certain writing upon it, which Mrs. Evoy swore was her penmanship."[19] The evidence, although circumstantial, was damning. At the end of the sheriff's interrogation Harper reportedly dropped into a chair and essentially confessed when he exclaimed, "I am ruined!"[20] Bridget's satchels of gold were returned to her intact. Harper had tangled with a member of society's "weaker sex" and had come out of it decidedly scathed. He was promptly jailed pending trial.[21] At the trial, Harper's lawyer ran through highlights of Harper's career and begged the jury to save his client from "ignominy and shame." In his own defense, Colonel Harper delivered a rambling, emotionally charged speech crafted to pull at the jurors' heartstrings and place a heavy burden on their consciences. A newspaper correspondent who attended the trial wrote:

> His appeals were most eloquent and brought tears to the eyes of many who listened to him. He seemed perfectly free from embarrassment during the delivery of his speech. He remarked that he stood alone, without friends, money, or influence. It would be a heart of stone that would not deeply sympathize with the prisoner when he alluded to his aged father and pious mother, under whose holy precepts and examples he had been nurtured and prayerfully admonished against the commission of evil deeds.[22]

The article went on to describe Harper's invocation of religious themes: "Breathless silence prevailed as he made this last appeal, and his last struggle for liberty commending himself to the mercy of the Jury and to God the friend of the lonely."[23] His impassioned, meandering arguments managed to avoid one crucial element: an explanation for the chain of incriminating evidence and his suspicious behavior at the time of the search. The jury was unmoved and found him guilty of grand larceny. The story made for sensational headlines in the newspapers of Northern California and even made it into the *New York Times*. Public sentiment was mixed, as many found it difficult to believe a prominent citizen and public servant would engage in such an unseemly act as to take advantage of and rob an older woman traveling alone in the rough-and-tumble northern mining region. The *New York Times* article expressed an incredulity shared by other correspondents who wrote of the notorious robbery: "The case is still involved in some doubts, and the accused may not be guilty."[24] Harper served seven years at San Quentin Penitentiary in Marin County until his prison sentence was commuted by Governor John Bigler on condition that Harper agree to leave the state of California.[25] Promptly upon his release from prison, Harper relocated to Nicaragua, where he lived for the remainder of his life.[26] The Bridget Evoy stage robbery story is repeated in the history compendiums for Trinity County and Butte County.[27]

In this period, Bridget sought to improve her California House hostelry, in the hope of keeping one step ahead of the competition. Malnutrition and illnesses such as scurvy were a persistent problem for miners living in the backwater mining districts, where the standard diet was heavy in meat, bread, and on very rare occasions, dairy. In the course of providing meals to the miners on a daily basis, she was well aware of this problem. Her travels by stage on the Marysville–Shasta route brought the acquaintance of William Myers, which led inadvertently to an opportunity. William Myers operated a roadside inn called Red Bluff House along the Marysville–Shasta Road.[28] Wishing to expand the fare served at his roadside inn, Myers and his wife planted vegetable gardens in the spring of 1851, but by the late spring of 1853, the gardens had failed. Myers's wife turned to Major John Bidwell and arranged to receive small shipments of vegetables from Bidwell's extensive gardens at his Rancho Chico estate, located on the Marysville–Shasta Road.[29] Subsequently, large baskets filled with peas, lettuce, turnips, cucumbers, carrots, and beets jostled around in the stage-coaches that made the runs along the route.

Learning of the Myers-Bidwell shipping arrangement, Bridget wrote Bidwell on June 13, 1853, requesting a line of credit to finance a supply of vegetables for the California House, "on the same terms as Mrs. Myers."[30] Her return address on the letter was noted simply as "Briggsville." Interestingly, the author Erwin Gudde used this letter as evidence of Briggsville being an early gold mining camp in his seminal book about the Gold Rush, *California Gold Camps.* With this shipping arrangement in place Bridget could offer her boarders fresh vegetables—a luxury in any mining community in the early 1850s, especially in a remote settlement like Briggsville. This novel and much-welcomed improvement to the fare offered at the California House set Bridget apart from her local competitors and helped to stave off the malnutrition that plagued her miner patrons. Throughout June and July, Bidwell continued sending shipments to Bridget by way of Hall & Crandall's US Mail Stage Line, which apparently did not object to transporting the vegetable-filled baskets. These shipments totaled 138 pounds of vegetables at a cost of $13.65. She and Ellen may have preserved or canned some of this produce for use in the winter months. Interestingly, Bidwell's shipments to Bridget continued nearly a month beyond the date (July 5) when Bidwell had notified Myers that the stage drivers were refusing to transport additional shipments to his Red Bluff House.[31]

Throughout her travels Bridget remained keen to receive intelligence on the mining districts and kept her ear to the ground, so to speak. She was typically quick to strike at promising opportunities if they appeared pragmatic. But sorting through the background noise, separating fact from rumor, was an eternal challenge. The mining camps within the northern goldfields were in continual flux, with boom-and-bust patterns being the order of the day. Those miners who failed to foresee opportunity or were reckless when they did achieve rare success were damned to a

Bridget's letter to Major John Bidwell requesting a vegetable shipping arrangement by stagecoach, 1853. John Bidwell Papers, 1841–1917, California History Room, California State Library.

hardscrabble existence, as the California historian Hubert Howe Bancroft described eloquently:

> The miners were a nomadic race, with prospectors for advance guard. Prospecting, the search for new gold-fields, was partly compulsory, for the over-crowded camp or district obliged the new-comer to pass onward, or a claim worked out left no alternative. But in the early days the incentive lay greatly in the cravings of a feverish imagination, excited by camp-fire tales of huge ledges, and glittering nuggets, the sources of these bare sprinkling precious metals which cost so much toil to collect.[32]

Bancroft continued, "Rumors of success are quickly started, despite all care by the finder to keep a discovery secret, at least for a time. The compulsion to replenish the larder is sufficient to point the trail and the fox-hound's scent for its prey is not keener than the miner for gold. One report starts another; and some morning an encampment is aroused by files of men hurrying away across the ridge to new-found treasures."[33] While casting a wide net among her sources, Bridget learned of the emerging mining settlement of Yreka, situated in the far northern reaches of the state in Siskiyou County. In a classic example of the mining boomtown phenomenon, gold was initially discovered there in 1851 at Black Gulch (later known as Thompson's Dry Diggings). The Yreka settlement quickly evolved into a robust mining community. Joaquin Miller, who visited the settlement in 1853–54, described it as a bustling place with "a tide of people up and down and across other streets, as strong as if in New York."[34] More stage lines maintained a stop in Yreka than in any other community in the state. Sensing opportunity, at Yreka Bridget purchased a parcel with a cabin on it. She most likely rented the cabin to locals, although she maintained a long-term goal of reselling the property when she perceived the local market was peaking, always an elusive target in the transitory mining region.

In the same summer of 1853, Zach Montgomery's activities in the Shasta–Clear Creek region were raising his public profile. Given his status and his residing at Shasta City, a mere five miles north of Briggsville, Bridget and Ellen were most likely aware of him by reputation but could not know that their paths would soon intertwine. At this time Zach mounted an unsuccessful bid as a Whig candidate for district attorney of Shasta County.[35] Among other ambitions, he turned his attention to the growth of the northern mining districts and began to advocate for much-needed improvements to the regional transportation infrastructure. He championed a proposal for a railroad route extending through the northern reaches of the Sacramento Valley, which would foster the permanence of some of the communities.[36] As part of this larger infrastructure proposal, Zach supported the establishment of a toll bridge over Clear Creek near Bell's Landing.[37] This bridge, funded in part by the county in the fall of 1853, subsequently became an important thoroughfare for miners and merchants accessing mining settlements such as Horsetown and Briggsville in southern Shasta County. Given the local demographic makeup dominated by individual miners and small-scale merchants, Zach's practice provided him with a very modest living. Deciding a change was in order, he relocated to a placer mining area along the Pit River in the Klamath Mountain region, and after spending a few months in another fruitless pursuit of mining, Zach concluded that "the elephant" of the argonaut would eternally allude him. The growing Marysville–Yuba City region to the south suggested greater opportunity for a law practice and, potentially, political office. In 1854 he relocated to Yuba City and established a law practice across the river in the more populated Marysville, which showed potential for a growing clientele.[38] Recently, Marysville had eclipsed Yuba City as a more practical setting for commerce because miners coming up the Feather River by boat embarked on the Marysville side, leaving Yuba City to stagnate as a commercial center. Like Ellen and Bridget, Zach preferred Marysville as a place to conduct business and promptly entered into a law partnership in the commercial center with Francis L. Aude. He became an influential member of the Marysville Bar, a professional association. In this year he met a local woman named Helena F. Graham, a recent arrival from Rochester, New York. A brief courtship followed and, on July 4, 1854, they married at Marysville and settled in Yuba City.[39] In December 1855 Helena gave birth to a son, Thomas Graham Montgomery.

Given the intertwining paths of Ellen, Bridget, and Zach in both Shasta County and the Yuba City–Marysville areas, it was natural that their paths would cross sooner or later. This acquaintance, coming almost randomly at first, would eventually have unforeseen and far-ranging consequences for all parties.

CHAPTER 8

This Pacific Eden

Rancho Encinal de Temescal

Delightful vistas, lovely slopes, beautiful groves, pleasant hillsides, a rich soil, abundant water and an inviting landscape, formed portions of the attractions presented by this Pacific Eden.

William Halley, speaking of Oakland

In the Clear Creek mining settlements of the Shasta region, the boom-and-bust patterns of economy, racial intolerance, and impulsive vigilante violence likely led to Bridget's growing weariness with life in the mother lode. These challenges were only punctuated by the attempted theft she endured at the hands of an allegedly honorable man, Colonel Harper. Despite her strong financial footing, she longed for a return to a simpler life, one like she knew in St. Louis and in Ireland. She may have missed the tangible rewards that came with living off the land and the pride she had taken in raising animals. Plus, being in her early sixties at this point, she undoubtedly felt the stamina required for life in the gold camps was becoming unsustainable. By the fall of 1853, she was formulating a new plan that would take her south to the San Francisco Bay Area.

Extending from the 1770s the territory's Hispanic inhabitants, the Californios, had enjoyed the fruits of the rich and varied landscape of grass-covered plains, great estuaries, and vast woodlands of the eastern shores of the San Francisco Bay Area, the "East Bay" in regional parlance. This rangeland was crucial for the maintenance of livestock, and hence their wealth was inexorably tied to owning expansive acreage, often awarded as land grants by the Spanish Crown or later, the Mexican government. Each rancho constituted a small fiefdom of sorts, with the don at the power center. However, the Gold Rush ushered in a period of major demographic, cultural, and environmental changes. Although by treaty with the Mexican government, the United States pledged to give Californios full rights as citizens and preserve their property ownership, once the influx of tens of thousands of settlers began, these promises fell by the wayside. Consequently, the days of Hispanic dominance in the region began to wane. New arrivals in Northern California and prospectors abandoning mining-based ventures in the Sierras were beginning to perceive the Bay Area not merely as a temporary waypoint or passing backdrop, but as a region primed for settlement, livestock ranging, and property investment. The waterway access to interior Northern California, the vast tracts of arable and pasturable land, and increasing land values were all factors that helped usher in a new era for the Bay Area as a land of promise. As settlers began to acquire farmland and establish fledgling communities, the land-use patterns in the region transitioned from livestock raising to crop cultivation. Western Contra Costa County and Alameda County were strategically situated within the region, within easy reach of shipping routes through the Golden Gate and the San Joaquin Delta.[1]

Bridget, who still owned residential parcels in San Francisco and at Santa Clara, also recognized this potential and soon turned her attention to the eastern shores of the San Francisco Bay, then the realm of a prominent Californio family, the Peraltas. The patriarch, Luis María Peralta, had accompanied Juan Bautista de Anza on his entrada to establish a mission and presidio at San Francisco. The Peraltas were the first non-Native people to settle the East Bay, on land granted by Pablo Vicente de Solá, the last Spanish governor of California, in 1820.[2] This grant, the 43,000-acre Rancho

San Antonio, encompassed a large portion of the East Bay in the Late Mexican period. Through the establishment of this and other massive Californio ranchos and their associated cattle ranging operations, native peoples were excluded from extensive swathes of traditional hunting-and-gathering lands. In 1836, Luis's son José Vicente and his wife, María, had established a homestead within the rancho along the north side of Temescal Creek, situated in the borderland bridging the modern cities of Berkeley and north Oakland. In 1842 Luis Peralta divided Rancho San Antonio among his sons, with José Vicente receiving the largest share. José Vicente Peralta's ranch encompassed a stretch along the bay waterfront known by the Californios as Contra Costa, or "other shore," because it lay opposite the bay's entrance at San Francisco. Of this tract, the historian William Halley noted, "Vicente retained not only the most eligible, but also the most beautiful of town sites. Delightful vistas, lovely slopes, beautiful groves, pleasant hillsides, a rich soil, abundant water and an inviting landscape, formed portions of the attractions presented by this Pacific Eden."[3] Vicente named his tract Rancho Encinal de Temescal.[4] The Mexican-era name for the adjacent creek, Arroyo del Temescal o Los Juchiyunes, appears to acknowledge the Indigenous Huchiun village within the watershed, which was presumably the source of the name.[5]

The Peraltas cultivated extensive wheat fields, fruit and nut orchards and, along the streamside terrace of Temescal Creek, fenced-in gardens, or *milpas*. They maintained vast herds of cattle, their primary resource for their domestic needs as well as trade (hides, tallow, and other products) with merchants who visited the bay in whaling ships. So important were the hides to the Californios that they were used as a source of currency and held value for trade and lines of credit.[6] The extensive slaughter yards, or *matanzas*, along Temescal Creek attracted winged scavengers from near and far as well as grizzly bears from the Contra Costa Hills (future Berkeley and the Oakland Hills).[7] The circling vultures over the matanzas acted like a beacon for the bears, who beat a path to the matanza for scavenging. This did not go unnoticed by visitors to the ranch. After a frightening encounter with a grizzly along Temescal Creek in the mid-1840s, William Heath Davis recalled being reassured by Peralta that "they [the grizzlies] were not hungry, having made a hearty supper from the slaughtered cattle." But Peralta offered an unnerving aside to his young visitor: "The bears were not to be trusted at any time. A youth of my fine appearance might be tempting to them."[8] The accounts of early East Bay explorers and settlers were rife with harrowing encounters with grizzlies.[9] Such was life in the then-rustic Contra Costa, long before the founding of the sprawling metropolis of Oakland, Berkeley, and Emeryville, presently home to millions.

The emergence of the communities of Oakland, Berkeley, Emeryville, and Piedmont commenced in 1850 with the activities of land speculators Horace Carpentier and partners Andrew Moon and Edson Adams.[10] They initially leased land from Vicente Peralta but soon begin selling 160-acre parcels within it. In the following year, 1851, the United States Land Act was passed, which required all holders of Spanish and Mexican land grants to present their titles for confirmation to a Land Claim Commission. Unless grantees presented evidence supporting their title within two years of the initial submission, the property would automatically pass into the public domain.[11] The requirements of the act placed a tremendous hardship on Mexican landholders, who had to hire lawyers to represent them against all comers, in some cases including hundreds of squatter claimants. Due to the financial pressures of fending off squatters on portions of Rancho Temescal, by 1852–53 Vicente Peralta had sold off all but seven hundred acres of his original rancho. Peralta and his fellow Californios faced an increasingly populous industrial society dominated by avaricious Anglo-American settlers who were driving the demand for land and natural resources.[12] These settlers were quickly transforming the previous frontier society into an industrial society. Mexican-origin citizens and Indigenous peoples continually adapted in an effort to survive, but the transformation of their world was brisk and unrelenting. The "Golden Age" of the

Californios was coming to its conclusion and, with it, the sun was setting on their way of life.

With the influx of settlers along the East Bay shoreline, the settlement at Contra Costa was organized in 1852 and officially renamed Oakland. The area that the Californios had traditionally called the Encinal ("Oak Grove") was translated loosely by the Euro-Americans as "Oakland" in the subsequent naming of the town. In his first address as mayor, Horace Carpentier emphasized its charms: "The chief ornament and attraction of this city consists, doubtless, in the magnificent grove of evergreen oaks which covers its present site and from which it takes both its former name of 'Encinal' and its present one of 'Oakland.'"[13] Through force of habit, the settlers were slow to adopt the new name, and the northern section around Temescal continued to be referenced locally and in legal documents as the "town of Contra Costa." In that year (1852), Contra Costa boasted seventy citizens, which doubled within a year. It hardly qualified as a village.

Sometime in the period Bridget traveled to the San Francisco Bay Area, probably on a business trip. Notably, she purchased a parcel in the Russian Hill district of San Francisco. Given her proclivity for purposeful movements within the region, she may also have been making a personal assessment of the area with her future in mind. Upon arriving in the fall of 1853, Bridget set her sights on a large parcel located within the Rancho Encinal de Temescal, just south of Vicente Peralta's homestead. The parcel that attracted Bridget's interest was located on "the road to Peralta" and owned by Jacob Tewksbury, a physician to the Castro family of San Pablo and a major landowner in Contra Costa County.[14] On December 9, 1853, Bridget purchased a ninety-seven acre-parcel from Tewksbury at a price of $3,000 in gold dust.[15] This property purchase established Bridget as an early pioneer of the Temescal settlement, one of the initial 140 residents of the future metropolis.[16] At the time of the property purchase, a farmer by the name of Lazarus McMakin was growing wheat on the acreage and, as part of the purchase, Bridget entered into an agreement in December to allow McMakin to lease the land in order to complete a harvesting cycle anticipated to take approximately one year. This offer of a lease to the sitting occupant of the purchased parcel was a method Bridget used in some of her property ownership arrangements. While waiting for the completion of the harvest at Temescal, Bridget commissioned the construction of a home, barn, and granaries using local redwood lumber. McMakin ultimately defaulted on the lease and Bridget sought compensation from Tewksbury, who was contractually obligated to compensate her if McMakin did not live up to the agreement. Tewksbury demurred and consequently, Bridget brought suit against him to recover her losses.[17]

In this period Bridget remained at Briggsville and, in response to a shifting marketplace, decided to repurpose her California House operation prior to sale. She had the building converted from a hostelry into a general merchandise store and venue for community events. By the mid-spring of 1854, she offered the establishment for sale, advertising it in newspapers throughout the northern mining region and Sacramento Valley. The newspaper advertisement, tailored to highlight the property's strategic value read, "To those wishing to engage in keeping a store and house of entertainment, a good opportunity is now offered; the above property is in the immediate vicinity of a rich mining country and possesses many varied advantages."[18] While the property was on the market, Bridget continued renting it for community events. In August 1854, the California House hosted a widely advertised social event, a "Cotillion Party," a forerunner of a square dance at which "a large number of ladies and gentlemen are expected to be in attendance."[19] These events drew attendees from the neighboring Clear Creek mining communities and Shasta City. People in this isolated area valued any opportunity to get to know one another, build community spirit, and perhaps initiate courtships among the younger set. Simultaneously, Ellen continued to broaden her financial horizons; she bought and sold commercial lots in Yuba County and acted as a property agent for Thomas Gilligan, a merchant who operated a wholesale

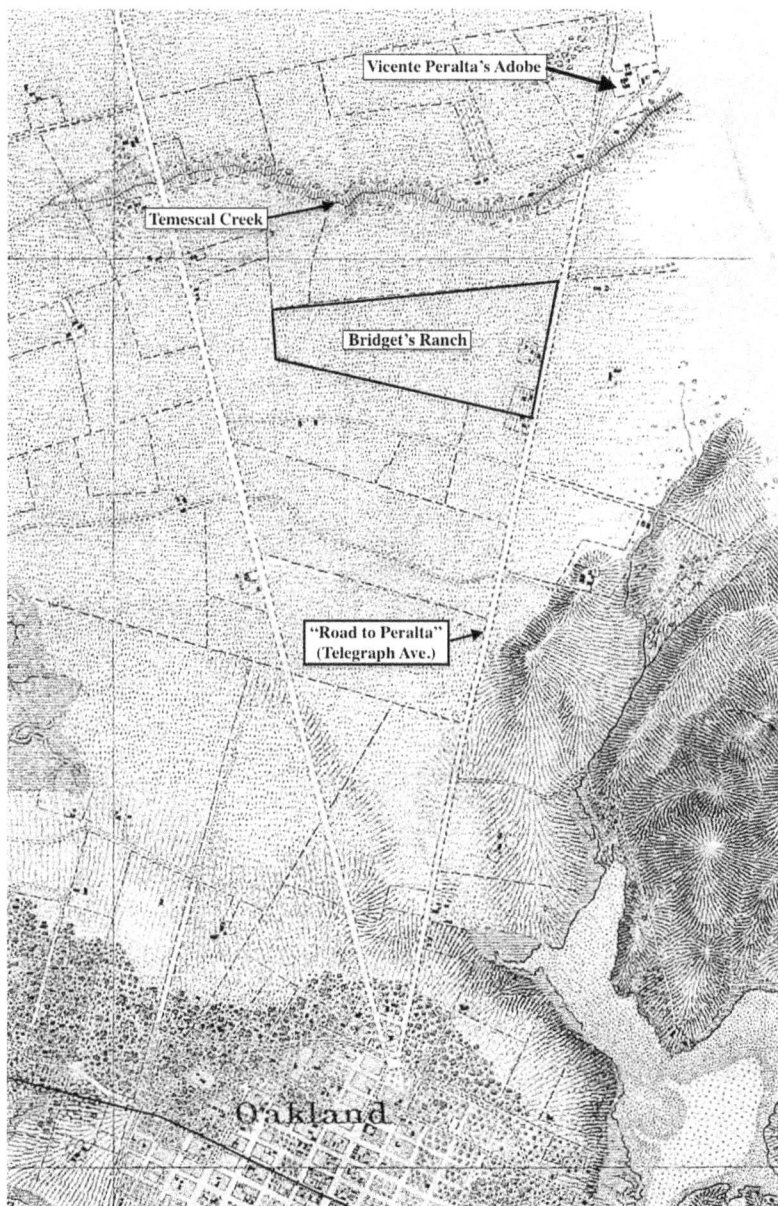

Map of the Rancho Temescal area, north of Oakland Township, 1859.
Courtesy of the Barry Lawrence Ruderman Map Collection, David Rumsey
Map Center, Stanford University Libraries.

dealer/retail store in Marysville.[20] Bridget and Ellen continued to use Briggsville as a base of operations throughout the first half of 1854, making occasional business trips by stage to Marysville, Yuba City, or Yreka and extended visits to Margaret at McCourtney's Crossing.

By the summer of 1854, Lazarus McMakin had vacated Bridget's Temescal property. Sometime that summer, she relocated to her new ranch. This departure from the mining region offered a respite from unrelenting labor and a time for reflection. For the first time in her adult life, she could reflect on the journey that had led to this place at this time. Her struggles to support her family in St. Louis, the life-threatening journey on the Overland Trail to the land of promise, and her resolve to gain independence in the tumultuous world of El Dorado had tested her mettle. Her unrelenting climb up the economic ladder meant she could finally return to a life tied to her roots and one that she valued more than any other, the life of a farmer and rancher. By relinquishing much of her business management duties to Ellen, she could develop her ranch and oversee its daily functioning. A later journal article describing the Temescal hamlet painted a picture of Bridget's ranch; "Mrs. Evoy has a pretty spot, with a collection of handsomely grown mountain pines, which add greatly to the beauty of the place."[21] With the assistance of hired help, she soon established extensive row crops of wheat and raised cattle, pigs, geese, and chickens.[22] She took pride in her success at breeding animals, dairy cows in particular, which she entered into agricultural contests. Bridget found common ground with the Peraltas through their Catholicism, made social calls to their home, and probably attended the Peralta family chapel for prayer on Sundays. This private chapel, built at the Peralta homestead sometime in late 1840s or early 1850s, was the first private place of worship in the East Bay Area. During these visits the Peraltas undoubtedly regaled Bridget with stories of the glory days of the Rancho Encinal de Temescal. She may have found the stories of grizzlies so recently raiding the matanzas along Temescal Creek as incongruous as it was unnerving. She need not have worried, for alas, the days of the mighty bruin marauding through the Encinal had passed.[23] At this time Temescal was entirely rural and only sparsely populated, with settlers maintaining large farms, growing grain and other products, and raising livestock. The northern hamlet was connected to the township of Oakland, an hourlong ride by horse to the south, via two rutted dirt roads: Peralta Road (future Telegraph Avenue) and San Pablo Road. Across the bay, meanwhile, San Francisco was also experiencing a pulse of growth

Portrait of Margaret McCourtney, circa 1870s. Although married and a mother of several children, Margaret was a prolific and versatile independent entrepreneur in Northern California in the latter half of the nineteenth century. Courtesy of Carol Glover.

as it steadily expanded westward of the civic center into an area called the Western Addition and Russian Hill. Margeret, seeing this opportunity, purchased a portion of Bridget's large parcel on Vallejo Street and Franklin Street in 1861. At this early date, this outlier of the city was primarily used for small-scale farming of row crops and orchards, but it would soon be sprouting houses.

Meanwhile, at McCourtney's Crossing, in addition to all her diverse business commitments Margaret was raising a large family of six young children, although by this time she typically had a live-in helper. The 1860 census for Yuba County gives an indication of the state of finances at the East Bear River Township. The McCourtneys provided the following figures for their jointly held assets: real estate valued at $15,000 and their personal estate at $10,500. Margaret also owned personal real property with a value of $2,000. She was identified as the sole owner of the general merchandise store and hostelry, whereas the ranch was jointly held by the couple.[24] At this time there were laborers and two thirteen-year-old Indians, Shandrack and Mathilda, living at the ranch.[25] The teenagers were most likely orphaned and came to the family through Catholic organizations who helped find placements for youths in unfortunate circumstances. They likely performed duties on the ranch or within the home. In the winter of 1861, the McCourtneys' bridge and most other bridges in the area were washed away by unusually heavy winter runoff triggered in part by the ongoing environmental impact of hydraulic mining and widespread timber harvesting. This was the second time the McCourtney bridge had been washed out in less than a decade. In 1862, a bill was introduced in the California State Senate to establish and finance a turnpike between Grass Valley and McCourtney's Crossing.[26] In the same period the governments of Nevada and Yuba Counties obtained an easement through McCourtney's Crossing for the construction of a replacement bridge, a cable-supported suspension bridge designed by Andrew Smith Hallidie.[27] Hallidie (1836–1900) was a prominent Californian inventor and bridge designer who made important contributions to the development of the suspension bridge in the United States. Hallidie referred to the new bridge at McCourtney's Crossing as "Bear River Bridge." Construction began immediately after the establishment of the 1861 easement and was completed in 1862 or 1863.[28]

In 1860 a new front of mining activity in the Bear River Township opened when copper-bearing deposits were discovered in the immediate area of McCourtney's Crossing. They included two significant leads of copper ore: the Distillery Ledge and the Diary Farm Mine.[29] These discoveries triggered a brief copper rush in the foothill region, leading to the establishment of the settlements of Sheridan and, several miles to the north, Smartsville to cater to the mining operations.[30] The increased local activity and toll traffic fostered the growth of McCourtney's Crossing. While John McCourtney was occupied with livestock ranging and other business ventures, Margaret began speculating in mining investments. Sometime in that period she bought shares in mineral mining ventures in Arizona (Tombstone Consolidated Gold and Silver Mining Company) and purchased stocks in a coal-mining venture in Washington state. Although married and engaged in joint ventures with her husband, she also entered into legal agreements in her own name. Influenced by her mother and sister Ellen, she would continue acting as a prolific independent financial player for the remainder of her life. Individually and as a team, Margaret and John McCourtney evolved into influential settlers and entrepreneurs within the Sacramento Valley/Sierra Foothills region. Their McCourtney's Crossing became a prominent historical landmark.

CHAPTER 9

Tapestry

All things are bound together, all things connect

Chief Seattle

While Bridget was settling into her Temescal farm, she continued buying, renting, leasing, and selling properties in several emerging communities in Northern California. At times she took out loans against the appreciated value of a property and used the cash to settle debts, make property improvements, or fund the purchase of other properties in promising settlements. In fact, in October 1857 Bridget took out a loan of $10,000 against the estimated or appraised value of her Temescal tract, undoubtedly the most valuable asset in her real property portfolio.[1] Although still living at the Bear River Township, by this time Margaret had also turned her attention to the growth potential of the Temescal district and, after some prompting by her mother, Margaret purchased a 58½-acre parcel located across the road from Bridget's Temescal ranch.[2] This tract would later serve as the hub of a new McCourtney headquarters. Throughout this period, Ellen continued to oversee Bridget's business interests in Yuba County (Marysville), Sutter County (Yuba City), Shasta County (Briggsville), and Siskiyou County (Yreka), as well as the residential lots in the Western Addition/Russian Hill district of San Francisco.[3]

Sometime in this period, John Evoy's reconnected with his extended family. An obscure character within the Evoy narrative, his movements and comments about him from various family members suggest he didn't maintain strong familial connections. After arriving in California about 1851, he engaged in mining in the northern mining districts in the early 1850s. The details of his movements in the gold region are lost to time but there is no evidence of his having made a success of it. It would seem he lacked the proactive and disciplined business acumen of Margaret, Ellen, or Bridget. On balance, the triumvirate posed by the Evoy women would have served as a very high bar for judging achievement. By January 1860, he had turned his attention to cattle ranging and settled on land within the Rancho Sobrante grant in Contra Costa County.[4] Their property was located within an area known colloquially as Cruzito Valley, within the San Pablo Creek drainage adjacent to the ranch of Victor Castro, the presiding Californio (as Mexican-origin residents of the California Territory were called) don of Rancho Sobrante.

Meanwhile, Mary Ann and Joseph Mullikin and their young children came out to California from St. Louis sometime about 1860. In December 1861 Bridget sold Margaret her property in the Russian Hill district of San Francisco, and Margaret then leased a portion to Mary Ann and Joseph, who chose to maintain their residence there. Looking to establish a financial foothold in the region, they soon entered into a livestock ranging venture with John Evoy in Contra Costa County. John, Mary Ann, and Joseph collectively established a ranch and ranged cattle over one hundred acres of the rolling hills along San Pablo Creek, several miles south of the settlement of San Pablo.[5] Census records for 1860 indicate John Evoy claimed land valued at $2,000 (real estate) and $2,000 in personal assets.[6] In about 1862 John married Mary J. Anderson, an Irish national who hailed from the town of Ardee, County Louth, Ireland. They settled in at their Cruzito Valley ranch.

Simultaneous with Ellen's business activities in the Yuba City/ Marysville community, Zach was establishing a reputation as an emergent legal mind, orator, and political leader in the northern counties of California. For the first time since arriving in the region, he began to enjoy a settled life, running a law practice in Marysville and living in Yuba City with his young wife, Helena and newborn son, Thomas. Yuba City was beginning a transition from a transitory jumping-off point into a more stable residential and commercial community, although it had yet to eclipse the growth of Marysville. Between 1856 and 1860 Zach served as district attorney of Sutter County, quickly establishing a reputation as a vigorous prosecutor.[7] Just as it appeared his career was blossoming, tragedy struck on July 18, 1856, when Helena died of an unspecified illness just eight months after giving birth to Thomas.[8] To take his mind off his pain, Zach immersed himself in his work with a renewed intensity and traveled extensively throughout the northern mining region on speaking tours. His beliefs about the need for reform of the state's public education system were near and dear to his heart and a subject he would write and speak about for decades. These tours brought him to the mother lode towns of Nevada City, Auburn, Columbia, Timbuctoo, and Coloma, and the northern towns of Shasta City and Oroville. Given the strong similarities in their respective movements within the northern counties over several years, it was almost inevitable that Zach's and Ellen's paths would converge. In addition to their similar and intertwining paths in the business world, both were quite active in the Catholic community of the gateway settlements. Sometime in early 1857, she and Zach began a courtship. Soon Zach proposed and in late April they made an extended visit to Bridget's Temescal ranch where they were married on April 28, 1857. Due to the friendship between Bridget and the Peraltas, Zach and Ellen were invited to hold their wedding ceremony in the private Peralta family chapel at Rancho Temescal, an honor afforded very few people outside the extended Peralta family.[9] With her marriage to this dynamic and well-connected man, Ellen's life would soon change considerably. They shared an assertiveness and an independent disposition. Zach and Ellen settled into a home on Second Street in Yuba City and, as he commenced his high-profile and storied careers in politics and law, they began a family of their own.[10] On February 15, 1858, Ellen gave birth to twin sons, John Joseph Montgomery and Zachariah Montgomery Jr.[11] Over the next couple of years, more children were born: Mary in 1859 and, remarkably, a second set of twins, Margaret and Ellen Rose, in 1861.[12]

Whereas Zach excelled at rhetoric and persuasion within legal and political forums, he was not generally a financially motivated person. Conversely, Ellen's sharp business acumen and pragmatic approach to pursuing her livelihood helped refine Zach's attitude toward that aspect of his life. Ellen, Margaret, and Bridget all exerted an influence and nurtured his tentative movements into business matters. Soon he began investing in commercial properties in Yuba City. In some of these investments, Zach partnered with Bridget, as he did in 1859 to buy the City Bar saloon in Yuba City from a colleague of Zach's for a nominal one dollar. Subsequently, they leased the saloon to its proprietor.[13] Their

Montgomery family, Christmas, 1858. Ellen and Zach hold (*left to right*), Zach Jr., John, and Thomas. Courtesy of Archives and Special Collections, Santa Clara University.

investment paid off handsomely six years later, in 1866, when they sold the commercial lot for $150.[14] Zach also became an important legal ally for Bridget and her daughters. While conducting his law practice and serving in political office, he occasionally fended off legal challenges over lease agreements and played a supportive role in their attempts to evict illegal squatters from some of Bridget's and Margaret's properties.

At the beginning of the twelfth session of the California Legislature (1860–61) Zach won a seat in the California State Assembly representing the Fifteenth District, which at the time included Sutter County.[15] Throughout the first half of the 1860s, the Civil War dominated state politics. As a constitutional scholar, Zach viewed the actions of the Lincoln administration through a legal perspective and, in particular, the Constitution. On the floor of the State Assembly and at public speaking engagements, Zach engaged frequently in heated debates with his characteristic animated, vigorous, and emotive speaking style. One editor, having witnessed some of Zach's more impassioned speeches, humorously described him as a "human calliope." Charles DeLong, a fellow assemblyman, referred to Zach as a "picturesque character" and a "southern firebrand" whose style of oratory he described as "howling."[16] However, Zach's leadership and skills of persuasion were recognized widely by his peers. In February 1861, he was given the honor of delivering the State of the Union address for the California Legislature.[17]

In December 1861, at a time when Zach and Ellen were enjoying their growing family and looking forward to the future, a sudden and tragic twist of fate unraveled their world. A brief warm spell following a rainy period in the Yuba area led to lush growth in the fields of Yuba City. Taking advantage of a break in the weather, two of the Montgomery children, Thomas and Zach Jr. ventured into the open field adjacent to their home, where the grasses and wild mushrooms attracted their interest. They sat in the dewy grass and ate some of the mushrooms. They quickly fell ill. As their symptoms worsened, a doctor was called and the family anguished in their helplessness as they prayed at the bedside. But as the hours passed, the doctor acknowledged there was little he could do. In the early morning hours of the following day, both children succumbed. The sudden loss devastated the young family and generated an outpouring of sympathy and support from the local community. Over the span of a few hours, the couple had lost two of their six children. Only Mary, John, Margaret, and Ellen Rose remained. Bridget came to stay with the Montgomerys to offer comfort and help with the children while Ellen grieved.

Despite their loss, throughout the period of 1861–63, the couple established themselves as prominent members of the Yuba City community, staying active in local civic, political, and church matters. At their home on Second Street, they entertained the leading members of local society. Ellen sponsored teas with prominent women and was active in the Catholic church and its missions. On any given evening, Zach might be found in the parlor of the Montgomery home, entertaining local politicians, clergy members, newspaper editors, authors, and other influential men from throughout the region. In April 1863 another son, Richard, was born.[18]

It was also at Yuba City where their oldest surviving son, John Joseph Montgomery, took an early interest in the celestial realm, a harbinger of things to come. John later recounted one of his earliest memories of the Yuba region, which instigated his interest in the then-visionary subject of flight. He obsessively watched the passing clouds and how they appeared to rest on Sutter Buttes, a prominent landmark a few miles northwest of the city. John recalled, "I thought that if I could get there, I could take hold of the clouds and fly; that I could grasp them and they would carry me with them. I think my interest in aerial navigation dates back to that time."[19]

By the end of 1863, Zach's public stance on the policies of the Lincoln administration began to impact his career. In October the US Congress and more than a dozen states loyal to the Union, enacted "loyalty oath legislation." Also called the "Test

Oath," this legislation cut across traditional boundaries of federal government authority to infringe on what traditionally were states' rights.[20] Being a strict believer in the Jeffersonian doctrine of states' rights, Zach refused to take the oath, for which he was forced to abandon the practice of law.[21] His disdain for the Lincoln administration grew, leading him to embark on extensive speaking tours throughout Northern California.[22]

In March 1864, the Montgomerys suffered the loss of a third child, Ellen Rose, who passed from an unknown childhood illness.[23] The loss was especially difficult for Ellen. As her mourning extended over the months, she began to associate their Yuba City homestead with personal tragedy. Reeling from the loss of both profession and family, the Montgomerys decided that a change of setting could bring healing. Bridget suggested they relocate to her ranch at Temescal. The notion of spending her remaining years surrounded by family may have appealed to her. In March 1864 the Montgomerys relocated to Oakland to live at the Evoy ranch.[24] Bridget, now seventy-three years old, was finding it difficult to keep up with the physical demands of travel to her far-flung business interests, and consequently, Ellen assumed more responsibility for carrying out Bridget's obligations. This included making occasional, arduous trips by stage to the northern counties. Bridget and her son-in-law Zach shared the common character traits of being highly individualistic, assertive, highly ambitious, and rarely thwarted in their professional pursuits. The close proximity of these two daunting personalities changed the family dynamic considerably.[25] Ellen was assisted in the home by a nanny, a necessity for a woman raising five children while managing a myriad of business responsibilities.

Once settled in the Bay Area, Zach established *The Occidental* newspaper in San Francisco, chiefly with a view to writing on the issue of public schools but also drawing attention to and criticizing the wartime policies of the Lincoln administration.[26] His published editorials and speeches solidified his reputation among his adversaries as an outspoken Southern sympathizer.

Montgomery home on Bridget Evoy's tract, Temescal district, Alameda County, California, circa 1868. Author's collection.

This would have personal ramifications. In the late spring of 1864, military authorities controlling the city under wartime restrictions began arresting without due process prominent citizens who spoke out against the Lincoln administration.[27] Outraged citizens organized a "Democratic Indignation Meeting" to be held in protest on August 3, 1864, at Hayes Park, San Francisco. Zach's status as a prolific orator and well-known critic of the Lincoln administration led to an invitation to speak at the protest rally. At the protest, Zach condemned the recent actions of the military in the city and, more broadly, the policies of the Lincoln administration. Emotionally charged rhetoric prevailed, and pro-Union newspapers strongly criticized the event. Zach received special attention from the editors of the *San Francisco Flag*, who accused him of treason and called for his arrest and hanging. As a reporter for *The San Francisco Daily Call*, Mark Twain also attended and wrote an article summarizing the protest rally. Twain wrote in part: "After the end of the music . . . Zach Montgomery, of Marysville appeared in the stand. . . . He commenced by saying that he would speak from the record (meaning that he would read a prepared speech)." Alluding to Zach's impassioned oratory and its intended effect of stirring up his audience, Twain, a master of wry humor, offered a classic Twainian aside, "after a little music to soften the lion which Montgomery had aroused (within himself) . . . Tom Robinson was presented."[28]

As President Lincoln campaigned for reelection in the fall of 1864, Zach's increasingly vitriolic anti-Lincoln editorials led to *The Occidental* being associated with the city's "Copperhead Rags," which collectively called for an immediate end to the war. When news of Lincoln's assassination reached San Francisco early on the morning of April 15, 1865, an angry mob formed and commenced violently ransacking the offices and printing facilities of the known anti-Lincoln newspapers. The offices of *The Occidental* and several other papers, including *The San Francisco Newsletter*, were looted and the presses destroyed.[29] The *Daily Alta California* reported, "just after 5.00 PM, the crowd entered the offices of The Occidental, a rabid succession weekly sheet of the existence of which, owing to its limited circulation, but few of this community knew. The office which was situated in the brick building was quickly gutted, and the material thrown out into the street and burned (including furniture and the printing press). A few more newspaper offices were spared from sure destruction by the arrival of some 50 troops armed with muskets and fixed bayonets."[30] According to oral family history, as the rioters approached the building that housed *The Occidental,* Zach grabbed some important papers and fled. Unrecognized as he passed the lead elements of the mob in the stairwell, he narrowly escaped a violent attack. Zach took a ferry across the bay to Oakland and, fearing reprisals from the public, he stayed at a neighbor's farm for several days to avoid risking a potentially violent scene at the family homestead at Temescal. A few determined people intent on confronting Zach visited the Evoy ranch and, failing to find him, attempted to bribe the Montgomery children with offers of candy if they would divulge Zach's whereabouts.[31] The children were told by Ellen and Bridget to feign ignorance. The fallout from Zach's activities created anxiety for the young family and further reinforced the importance of a protective family environment. Despite her assertive nature, Bridget could not influence her equally strong-willed son-in-law's public opinion campaigns for certain causes. What must she have thought of Zach's bringing tension into her formerly peaceful ranch?

Still, despite the disruption Zach caused, the relocation of the young Montgomery family to the Temescal ranch gave Bridget a new purpose as the doting grandmother to the Montgomery brood. In the evenings, Bridget held court over the children at story time as she rocked in her cherished rocking chair, a Rococo Revival piece made very popular after the assassination of Abraham Lincoln, who owned an almost identical chair.[32] Always the vehement Lincoln critic, Zach might have disliked the sight of the indomitable family matriarch seated in a Lincoln Rocker regaling his children with bedtime stories of Irish folktales, the Overland Trail, the nearly fatal Sierran crossing in the winter of 1849, the colorful characters in the mining camps, and perhaps the bold theft of her gold by Colonel Harper and her ultimate victory over him. But, watching the children sprawled on the buffalo rug hanging on to Bridget's every word, Zach might have concluded that the Lincoln Rocker could be acceptable after all.

CHAPTER 10

Passing of the Matriarch, End of an Era

Tá an saol ag athrú i gcónaí, cosúil leis an t-aistriú sa chior-
cal Ceiltiach

    *Life is constantly changing, like the turning in the Celtic
circle.*

Gaelic proverb

Throughout the late 1850s and the 1860s Bridget was living the
life of a gentlewoman farmer. She had gained financial stability,
built a network of influential contacts throughout the region and
as a consequence reached the highest echelons of society. However, never a player in elite social circles nor prone to displays of
wealth, she was drawn to the earthbound pleasures of ranch life
in the Temescal district. Although considered an elderly woman,
she remained vigorous in her daily life. She served as ranch boss,
overseeing the daily duties of the ranch hands and assisting in the
care of the livestock.

    The 1860 population census, taken that summer, revealed her
progress at Temescal:[1]

value of the land: $10,000
value of personal estate: $3,000
acres improved: approximately 100
cash value of farm: $10,000
value of farming implements/machinery: $200

animals: 2 horses, 2 cows, 50 pigs, unenumerated goats,
   chickens, and geese
value of livestock: $600
grains in storage: 2,000 bushels of wheat and 2,500 bushels
   of oats

This represents an impressive increase in property value in
seven years, from $3,000 in 1853 to $10,000 by 1860, a reflection
of her prescience in seeing the growth potential of this future
quaint suburb of Oakland. Bridget took pride in her animals and
occasionally entered her milk cows in livestock contests at various fairs. At Temescal the horses alternated between pulling the
ploughs and the spring wagon for trips to the Oakland township.
Her extensive farm was a self-sustaining operation financed in
part through the cultivation of oat and wheat for sale at the end
of each year's harvest cycle. Once harvested, the grain crops were
stored in large sheds until they could be sold to a middleman.
The sold crops were either milled and used locally or shipped by
wagon to the railroad wharf at Oakland and loaded on ships for a
marketplace elsewhere.

Bridget put her personal stamp on her ranch by designating
the road bordering the south edge as Rosegarland Way, a nod to
her native Irish village. A road bordering her parcel to the north
was designated Ellen Street.[2] An ardent, lifelong equestrian, she
usually took to horseback when running errands in Oakland
Township or visiting socially with neighbors on other ranches,
such as the Peraltas' Temescal rancho.

Although Bridget had never engaged directly in mining, her
interest in the subject had always been keen. This interest inspired
mischief by her grandson John J. Montgomery. John's sister Jane
recalled a practical joke that he played on his grandmother. Bridget's laborers (John Brient and the Indian Charley) were plough-
ing the grainfields at her ranch. As Jane later recalled, "When the
men were at lunch, John, armed with a little cannon he had constructed, loaded it with blueing balls (laundry blueing) and shot

Bridget Miranda Evoy, circa mid-1850s. Courtesy of Carol Glover.

his cannon along the newly ploughed furrows." John McCourtney had told Bridget of encountering blue clay in association
with gold-bearing placers on his Nevada City mining claim, a
story young John Montgomery evidently recalled. Jane continued, "When grandmother saw the blue deposit on the furrows,
she became very much excited—thought there must be some new

mineral in the soil and immediately ordered specimens sent to be assayed—Johnny kept MUMB [sic.]"[3]

As nod to his mother's and grandmother's Irish roots, young John Montgomery constructed an aeolian harp, which he installed in the upstairs window of the family's Temescal home. An aeolian harp, or "wind harp," is activated when a breeze causes the strings to vibrate, creating a harmonic tone. When the onshore breeze blew off the nearby bay and into the windows of the home, the strings would vibrate, producing an ethereal, haunting tone throughout the upstairs of the home.[4] For his doting Irish grandmother Bridget the sound may have evoked childhood memories of her life in the Irish hamlet of her youth.

Intellectually inclined from an early age, John became enamored with science and natural phenomena such as the flight of birds. Through his observations, he noted that, although birds were many times denser than air, they could fly nonetheless. How was that possible? he wondered. He later recalled his thinking at this early stage, "It has always seemed to me that the secret of aerial navigation lay in the discovery of the principle of a bird's flight—that the successful airship would not be modeled on the balloon nor dependent on its buoyancy." This conundrum could only be solved through systematic investigation. Birds in the wild were sufficiently elusive that he couldn't get close enough to see the motions of their wings in flight, so he came up with an ingenious plan for observation that required the unwitting participation of Bridget's geese: "The flying of wild geese interested me in consequence and as I couldn't get near enough to them for close and careful observation, I taught my grandmother's flock of geese to fly. I used to drive them down to the extreme end of the ranch and then by cracking a whip behind them compel them to rise and fly to the other end of the ranch." Speaking to an interviewer about the early memory, John chuckled as he recalled Bridget's reaction, "I think it was always a matter of wonderment to my grandmother why her geese could fly so much farther and better than her neighbors'."[5]

With the northward expansion of Oakland and the emergence of several fledgling communities around the city's boundaries (future Berkeley, Piedmont, Emeryville, and so on), civic leaders foresaw the need for a transportation system that could provide the growing Alameda County population with convenient access to San Francisco, by this time the major center of commerce in Northern California.[6] Temescal was centrally located within this growing region, and Telegraph Road served as a crucial artery for transportation between Oakland and the agricultural tracts of the northern hamlets of the East Bay waterfront. Bridget had been considering how Temescal might be served by an improved transportation system but did not agree that the complicated ferry boat–electric trolley system championed by politicians was the answer. She envisioned a rail service extending across the bay via trestle bridge and connecting the passenger terminals at the Oakland waterfront with San Francisco. Given the state of the region's resources and the will of civic leaders, this idea was more visionary than practical. So local politicians prevailed and, beginning in 1863, the San Francisco and Oakland Railroad Company established a steam train service extending from the downtown district to Oakland Point, where passengers boarded the ferry *Contra Costa*, bound for San Francisco.[7] With this development, Bridget saw that extending a steam rail spur through Temescal would place the hamlet centrally within a larger through-going transportation system, a potent idea for raising the value of her real estate. It was this intersection between population growth, transportation infrastructure, and land values that Bridget saw as vital to the future of the community and an idea that she had repeatedly used with some success at Marysville and at Briggsville, and that Margaret had used effectively at the Bear River Township. To that end, in early 1865, Bridget and Margaret joined forces to entice civic leaders to extend a new rail spur adjacent to their tracts, where it would connect with an existing rail line along Telegraph Road. For this purpose, Bridget transferred to the City of Oakland a one-hundred-foot lane following the former

Rosegarland Way east–west on a direct line from Market Street to Telegraph Road. Simultaneously, Margaret transferred to the city a portion of Rosegarland Way bordering the southern boundary of her large tract.[8] The rail spur idea languished for several years before eventually being realized.

The spring of 1865 saw the birth of Bridget's youngest grandson, James P. Montgomery.[9] Only a few months after it began, James's life nearly came to an abrupt end. On October 8, 1865, the first so-called Great San Francisco Earthquake struck the Bay Area.[10] According to family oral history, the infant James was in a bassinet placed on a chair in the kitchen when the earthquake hit. As the home began to thrust violently from side to side, the chair was thrown over. He hit the floor and rolled beneath the heavy, wooden kitchen table. The thick plaster ceiling partially collapsed and, as clouds of choking dust swirled throughout the home, Bridget and Ellen frantically groped through the debris-strewn kitchen in search of the infant, fearing the worst. Hearing James crying, they found him beneath the kitchen table, which had somehow resisted collapse when the plaster slabs falling from the ceiling landed on it.[11] Were it not for the table, the Montgomerys would have had to endure the unbearable pain of losing another child.

By the summer of 1867, Bridget's health was becoming increasingly frail. This led to extended hospital stays at St. Mary's Hospital in San Francisco, and by July it was becoming clear to family and friends that the indomitable matriarch was fading. She made out her will on July 30, 1867.[12] After an extended illness, she succumbed on December 3, 1867, her compelling life story reaching its natural conclusion. Hers was a life well lived and of consequence. As a courtesy, the Peraltas allowed her to be interred on a portion of their large cemetery plot in the historic St. Mary's Cemetery, situated on a ridgetop within the foothills of Oakland's Rockridge district. It is no coincidence that the ancient inhabitants of Ireland, the Celts, typically chose prominent hilltop sites for burying important members of their community. These burial sites, or barrows, typically overlooked landmarks of spiritual significance to the community. Bridget's final resting place overlooks her Temescal ranch and, quite appropriately, offers a sweeping view of the storied entrance to the San Francisco Bay, the Golden Gate. The distant, oft fog-shrouded gateway to the bay represented the threshold to a land of promise and perhaps a symbolic reminder of Bridget's risky gambit for renewal and opportunity in the West.

To memorialize the family matriarch, a large white marble slab inscribed with her likeness (Bridget, rosary in hand, deep in prayer) marks her grave. The inscription reads:

> Sacred to the memory of B. M. Evoy, who was born at Rosegarland, County of Wexford, Ireland, A.D. 1791 and departed this life Dec. 3, A.D. 1867 at her residence in Oakland Township, Alameda County. Aged 76 years. Ripe in years and virtue, she sank to sleep, surrounded by her children and grandchildren to whom she bequeathed the priceless inheritance of an example, radiant with deeds of justice, benevolence, charity, and true Christian piety. May she and all the souls of the faithful departed, through the mercy of God, rest in peace, amen.[13]

The inscription highlighted in idealistic terms what Bridget symbolized to her daughters: a beloved mother, a woman of devout faith, and someone who led by example. It could be said that Bridget's fiercely independent attitude, her facility in carving out a life of consequence on her own terms, and her leadership inspired two or three generations of women in her family.

Bridget's will designated her sole male heir, John, as the executor of her estate, responsible for the dispersal of her real properties, cash, and other assets to her heirs. This would be a customary role for the oldest male child, but given the family dynamic, one might have expected Ellen or perhaps Margaret to be given this responsibility. As her Irish forebears would have done, Bridget

Marble memorial to Bridget Evoy on McCourtney family mausoleum, St. Mary's Cemetery, Oakland, California. Author's collection.

divided her ninety-seven-acre tract in Temescal among her living children: 13½ acres to John Evoy, 23 acres to Margaret McCourtney, 15 acres to Mary Ann and Joseph Mullikin, and 21 acres plus Bridget's house to Ellen Montgomery (added to the 30 acres sold to Ellen three years prior). As Bridget's primary business partner, Ellen also received Bridget's assets in Marysville (a home and land), a home and land in Yreka, and 50 percent of her property in the city of Santa Clara. Bridget left $300 to her sister Margaret Shannon, and several thousand dollars to be equally divided among her heirs. Interestingly, although she had numerous grandchildren, Bridget specifically named only one child in her will: her granddaughter Mary Ann McCourtney, to whom she bequeathed $300 in gold coin. Mary Ann was the little girl who rode in the saddlebag mounted on a mule through the Overland Trail journey in 1849. In this symbolic gesture, Bridget showed special affection for Mary Ann, with whom she had shared that harrowing and life-changing experience. Bridget made clear her intentions when she named each of her daughters in her will, sometimes adding "and her heirs." Through this mechanism, her daughters were given a clear line of succession and could not be deprived of financial opportunity by a present or future husband. In keeping with the theme of her adult life, her last wishes reflected her belief that women should be allowed to determine their own livelihood and their own life's course.

As her family grieved their loss and pondered the larger symbolism of Bridget's life and passing, the winds of change were being felt. All roads were leading to Temescal.

CHAPTER 11

Winds of Change

The longest way around is the shortest way home

Irish proverb

As a consequence of Bridget's passing, her children and their families were drawn to Oakland, where they settled on portions of the original ninety-seven-acre Evoy tract. John and Mary J. Evoy settled in the western part while Ellen and Zach lived in the eastern section. Mary Ann and Joseph Mullikin relocated to a portion of the Evoy tract but maintained livestock rangeland at Cruzito Valley on San Pablo Creek, as did John Evoy. Bridget's passing may have come at a time when Margaret had been considering a change. Despite the McCourtneys' long history of successful commercial ventures and investments in the mother lode, one outcome of living in this remote area of the foothills was crime. Their location along an important thoroughfare to the gold settlements brought them in contact with a wide variety of people, while at the same time, their isolation left them vulnerable. Some of the men coming through the crossing were marginal characters on the lookout for opportunity or beating a path away from the settlements to avoid suspicion of or punishment for some nefarious deed.

Given the setting and circumstances, it was inevitable that, sooner or later, crime would come knocking at their door, both figuratively and literally. On one occasion, Margaret had to travel into Marysville, which would require an overnight stay in town. Because there was a laborer or two living on the ranch, she may have felt safe leaving Mary Ann at home and in charge of the younger children (Margarette and Paul) in her absence. Sometime that evening, a loud banging commenced on the front door, which Mary Ann understood to be caused by a man, and by the tone of his voice, an angry one. Mary Ann, in her mid-teens at the time, decided it would be safer to pretend no one was home, so she did her best to quiet the children, but to no avail. Hearing a female voice coming from inside, the intruder continued pounding on the door, becoming increasingly agitated and determined to engage. Her fear rising with the growing cacophony, she concluded he was mad with drink and potentially violent. She corralled the children and pushed them beneath the bed, her thoughts racing in a desperate search for a way out of the situation. The ranch laborers were apparently out of earshot, and she assumed she was on her own. The stranger climbed onto the eaves of the roof, where the roof was lower and, having picked up a tool, began lifting roof shingles and then roof boards, determined to get into the home, or at least to create a hole large enough that he could reach in and unlock the door from the inside. Realizing she was in deep trouble and aware there was little chance of help coming, Mary Ann considered her next move. As the man pried off more roof boards, she could now see part of his flannel shirt. Panicky and in the grips of a primal drive for survival, she scanned the room and eyed the large butcher's knife on the kitchen counter. She saw her way out, and it was going to be ugly. She shoved the dining table beneath the now-gaping hole in the ceiling, grabbed the knife, climbed up on the table, and thrust the knife upward twice through the opening, sinking it deep into the man's shirt. He groaned in anguish and rolled off the roof, landing hard on the ground. Petrified, she crawled beneath the bed with the toddlers and cowered, waiting for what might come next. But only silence came, an excruciatingly long silence. Mary Ann kept vigil throughout the long, restless night, waiting anxiously for the break of daylight. She eventually found the nerve to peer out the door and then, after some hesitation, stepped out front, seeing no sign of the man. She waited for her mother to return.[1]

Another incident, unnerving for John and Margaret not because of its outcome but because of its boldness, occurred in early January 1868. The family and friends were having dinner at their residence when two strangers entered the home. Hooded and brandishing knives, they demanded money. A contemporary newspaper article described the incident: "notwithstanding the presence of five or six able-bodied men, [the intruders] robbed Mrs. McCourtney of $200 in coin and a gold watch."[2] This incident and other robberies and episodes of violence in the area around the same time precipitated a major change for the McCourtneys. There were important matters to attend to in executing Bridget's estate, and Margaret already owned a large tract in Temescal that could serve as a new homestead. Consequently, the McCourtneys settled their affairs in Yuba County and relocated to Margaret's land in the East Bay.

In the period after Bridget's passing, her complex estate languished unsettled for months under John Evoy's oversight, or lack thereof. At the time of probate (April 6, 1868), the total value of Bridget's estate within Alameda County was $43,800, or nearly $1 million in 2024 dollars.[3] John Evoy provided the following estimates of the value of Bridget's assets in Alameda County, which apparently did not include her other properties dispersed across several counties in Northern California:

real estate holdings: $40,000
income from rents, profits, and issues: $800
personal property $3,000

In Margaret McCourtney's and Ellen Montgomery's estimation, Bridget's estate was an important reflection of her achievement and her life's legacy extending back to the time of her arrival in the California Territory nearly twenty consequential years earlier. Concluding that John was failing to meet his obligations in administering the estate (paying out debts, maintaining financial records, and distributing Bridget's assets), they became increasingly concerned that Bridget's financial legacy would falter through his inaction. This led to confrontations between Margaret and her brother John. The Montgomerys and McCourtneys were loath to see Bridget's legacy squandered, but John appeared to have an ally in his sister Mary Ann and her husband Joseph Mullikin, his partners in the Cruzito Valley ranching operations. John McCourtney stepped in to act as an intermediary between the heirs in an attempt to resolve the conflict with John Evoy. The failure of his efforts led to a difficult decision for the remaining family members. In the spring of 1868, Margaret and John McCourtney petitioned the court to remove John Evoy as administrator and assign "Z. Montgomery or some suitable person" as executor and to act as their attorney. Zach wrote a petition to the court (cosigned by Margaret and Ellen) that was as stark as it was blunt. Never one to mince words, Zach asserted that John Evoy had struggled for several years with a debilitating alcohol habit that, among other consequences, impaired his judgment. In short, it was alleged that he had proven to be an incompetent administrator of this major estate. The petition insinuated John was not acting in good faith in his position of financial responsibility and was benefiting personally through avoiding the dispersal of the assets.[4] The heirs may have believed he would squander the assets and leave the estate exposed to fines and other financial penalties. With these assertions, a rift was opened within the extended family. Ellen and Margaret were entrenched on one side, John Evoy and Mary Ann Mullikin on the other. The case was finally settled when the court awarded John Evoy sole administration of the estate on May 6, 1868, and the collective heirs came to an agreement on the distribution of the assets on January 10, 1870. However, the acrimony within the family simmered without resolution.

Bridget's bequests to Margaret and Ellen did not substantially increase their wealth, as they each had cultivated successful business careers of their own. Conversely, the assets received by John Evoy and Mary Ann Mullikin changed their lives significantly, and in relatively short order. Given the comparative growth in land values between rural Contra Costa County versus the burgeoning northern reaches of Oakland, John's and Mary Ann's newfound wealth was far above and beyond what they would have achieved through ranching or through selling their Cruzito Valley ranch property. The inheritance of portions of the Evoy tract significantly uplifted their status financially and socially. As evidence of this, a comparison of John Evoy's assets pre- and post-inheritance is instructive. At the time of the 1860 census, John estimated the value of his rangeland in rural Cruzito Valley at $2,000. Ten years later (2½ years after Bridget's passing), after continued growth of the Oakland region, the value of John Evoy's inherited real estate holdings at Oakland was estimated at $100,000. After John's untimely passing in 1873, his widow, Mary J. Evoy, subdivided the John J. Evoy tract and began selling individual lots, a particularly lucrative practice.[5] Over the succeeding two decades, as the heretofore sleepy hamlet of Temescal filled in with residential and commercial developments, Mary J. Evoy emerged as perhaps the wealthiest of the extended family. At the time of her passing in 1894, Mary's estate (primarily real property) was estimated at between $250,000 and $300,000.[6]

After selling their property and businesses in Yuba County in the summer of 1869, the McCourtneys finally joined the extended family by relocating to the Temescal district.[7] Following a familiar pattern, Margaret continued to build her real property portfolio while John focused on developing their rural properties for livestock ranging and crop cultivation. Margaret purchased an eighty-four-acre tract within El Sobrante Rancho in Cruzito Valley, adjacent to the ranch of John Evoy and Mary Ann. Apparently by this time, a reconciliation of sorts had occurred between John and Margaret. Margaret saw additional opportunities for investments elsewhere. By the late 1860s, the Sacramento–San Joaquin River Delta region was becoming appreciated by farmers

Sacred Heart Catholic Church, on Bridget Evoy's tract, Temescal district, circa 1876. It was built with substantial support from Zach and Ellen Montgomery and Margaret McCourtney. Author's collection.

and real property investors and ranchers as a developable region.[8] The delta's freshwater tidal wetlands, situated at the confluence of these two major rivers, had traditionally been regarded as "barren wastes." However, draining the wetlands could reclaim the land as arable. Consequently, beginning in the late 1860s, levees were constructed, and water was drained from the marshlands to create grazing pasturage for livestock.[9] The State of California offered the delta region wetlands for sale to the public as "swamp and overflowed lands."[10] Margaret purchased a large tract of reclaimed land in her name on Sherman Island (Swamp Land Reclamation District No. 341). Here, John and one of his sons, Alfred, ranged cattle and grew hay on a large scale. Due to the natural sloughs that crossed their land, they had the luxury of having schooners call at their landing for shipping the hay.[11]

In this same period, urbanization of the East Bay increased dramatically after Oakland became the western terminus of the Transcontinental Railroad in 1869. Not surprisingly, Oakland's population swelled. In that year, the Oakland Railroad Company extended a line of horse-drawn streetcars from Oakland toward Berkeley via Telegraph Road, terminating at 40th Street bordering the south side of Bridget's tract.[12] The city directory boosted this route, noting, "The benefit of such improvements is very great, a population of several hundred persons having been drawn to the vicinity of Temescal through the influence of the Oakland Railroad." Around the terminus of the horsecar line grew a small business district."[13] Bridget had long anticipated this extension of transportation into Temescal and its potential to foment local commerce, residential patterns, and land values. The extended family members all took advantage of this improvement, establishing various businesses along Telegraph Road, including a law office (Zach), real estate office (Richard J. Montgomery), a carpentry and blacksmith shop (John McCourtney), and a general merchandise store (James and John Montgomery). This allowed them to attract business from the main thoroughfare fronting their properties and to engage in their livelihoods without the need to commute.

Beginning in the early 1870s, Zach and Ellen began subdividing portions of their tract and, in 1875, they offered twenty half-acre-sized lots for sale. A newspaper notice described the amenities of the location:

> The site is an attractive one, situated as it is on the northwest corner of Telegraph Road and Evoy streets, and is adjacent to the residence of Hon. Zach Montgomery, and includes his valuable orchard. Its commanding position upon the main avenue connecting the main portion of Oakland with the State University at Berkeley, and the

frequent communications by means of horse-cars, which pass every fifteen minutes, together with the fine view render the property very attractive for residence purposes and will cause it to enhance rapidly in value.[14]

In this period John McCourtney's blacksmith shop, located across the road from the Montgomery ranch, received daily visits from McCourtney's nephew, John Montgomery. Through these interactions the young inventor received important training in the basics of carpentry and blacksmithing from his uncle. Montgomery would later use these skills to construct mechanical experimental devices, and more importantly, a series of flying machines that he flew in the 1880s.[15] In fact, one of the more obscure facts in the annals of the history of technology is that the Temescal district of Oakland (specifically the Evoy and McCourtney tracts) served as "fertile ground" for the invention of human flight.

Once settled in Temescal, the McCourtneys' progress was impressive, with Margaret holding their Alameda County assets in her own name. The US population census recorded Margaret's assets within Alameda County in 1870 as consisting of real property valued at $40,000 and a personal estate worth $3,000.[16] Her larger business interests, spanning numerous ventures scattered across Northern California and in mining operations in the broader West, were worth considerably more. At this time, she was identified personally in the tax records as one of the largest landowners in the East Bay and the Sacramento–San Joaquin River Delta regions, typically labeled on the regional landowner maps as "Mrs. M. P. McCourtney." In terms of her social connections, Margaret was by any standard a member of upper-class circles. Ellen was similarly situated socially. But, coming from a working-class background, these pragmatic, self-made Evoy women would hardly engage in conspicuous displays of wealth or embrace attitudes that can emerge with privilege. Margaret's attitude remained unaffected by her financial success. She continued to engage in farming on her Temescal tract. She acquired a real estate license and ran a real estate business out of an office on Telegraph Road at 42nd Street, focused largely on selling small residential lots within her large Temescal property. Through this mechanism she could exert greater control over her property transactions.

Throughout her life Bridget had never forgotten the poverty that plagued the Ireland of her youth and the hardships she had faced as a widowed mother to five children on the Missouri frontier. She understood what it meant to have nothing, to extract a paltry living off the land, and to face a dismal future. She encouraged her daughters to show compassion toward those who were less fortunate and to help where possible. As the Evoy daughters consolidated their financial successes and matured, they contributed to their community in important ways. Zach's entrance into the family brought his important connections to the Catholic Church hierarchy in the state. In 1849 Zach's uncle Charles Pius Montgomery, a prominent Dominican priest in Ohio had been appointed as the first Catholic bishop of the Californias (Baja and Alta). He had to decline the appointment due to his ailing health, and Joseph S. Alemany was chosen to serve instead. Through Catholic-based social activism, the extended Evoy/McCourtney/Montgomery family sought to support and uplift the poor and disabled. Seeing a need for a local Catholic parish in the community of North Oakland, in the mid 1870s Ellen and Margaret, with support from Archbishop Joseph Alemany, championed a new Catholic mission there.[17] To support this effort they dedicated a portion of the Montgomery/Evoy and McCourtney tracts in the Temescal district and helped establish the Sacred Heart Parish. The parish was officially established on January 13, 1876, but as no church had yet been built for the nascent congregation, the first mass was held in the parlor of Zach and Ellen's home on January 19, 1876. The McCourtneys and Montgomerys helped organize fundraising events and contributed money for the erection of a church.[18] Sacred Heart Catholic Church was dedicated by Archbishop Alemany on December 17, 1876, administered by a priest transferred in for the purpose, Father Lawrence Serda. In that year, a small school associated with the new parish was erected on a portion of the Montgomery tract, built and equipped by the Montgomery family and under the supervision of Father Serda.[19]

In early 1880 the parish's educational efforts expanded when Father Serda, with the support of Archbishop Alemany, established the St. Lawrence School on Evoy Avenue, a school for girls taught by the Sisters of the Holy Names of Jesus and Mary. Although a parochial Catholic school, admission was reportedly open to girls of all Christian denominations.[20] In the first year, the school's attendance grew from fifty-six pupils to more than one hundred, ranging in age from six to nineteen years. Margaret would later (in the mid-1890s) donate a portion of her Temescal tract to the diocese for the establishment of the Deaf-Mute Institute run by the Sisters of St. Joseph. Lacking an endowment and almost wholly dependent on charitable donations, the home was never able to support large numbers, but its influence among the adult deaf community through the St. Francis de Sales Society was widespread in the city and larger region.[21] Bridget's support for the Sisters of St. Joseph's mission had extended back to her days in St. Louis in the 1830s and 1840s.

The younger generations were encouraged to assume the family mantle of pursuing commercial enterprise. Ellen encouraged her three sons, John, Richard, and James Montgomery, to follow in her footsteps and engage in business, with greater or lesser success than she had. After graduating from St. Ignatius College at San Francisco in 1880, John languished as an editorial assistant for his father Zach's quarterly journal, *The Family's Defender Magazine and Educational Review*. Bored and restless, John was ill-suited for the task. Sensing that John needed to initiate an independent career, Ellen went to great lengths to set him up to follow the family tradition of commercial ventures. She paid for the construction of a general merchandise store (Montgomery Bros.) on the Evoy/Montgomery tract fronting Telegraph Road. John tended the register while his teenage brother James ran deliveries to local customers in Temescal.[22] Headed by an undermotivated manager, the Montgomery Bros. commercial venture was unsurprisingly brief. Conversely, Richard showed a natural facility for business. He would eventually become an important real estate developer and major booster for the Temescal district, which he actively promoted throughout the 1890s and thereafter as "Central Oakland." Using transportation infrastructure as a real property marketing angle, Richard subdivided the former Evoy tract into small residential and commercial lots. A later published biography noted that Richard was "regarded as one of the substantial and reliable businessmen of his city and, through his activities as a realtor, has contributed in large measure to the development and upbuilding of this district."[23] Richard, like his mother and grandmother, also offered loans for real property transactions. He has been credited for opening the real estate market within the Temescal district following its annexation by the City of Oakland in 1897.[24]

Replacing the city's outmoded steam-driven and horse-drawn streetcars, in the early 1890s the Oakland Consolidated Street Railway began running electric streetcars along its Key Route. Adopting the city easements established by Bridget and Margaret in 1865, the Key Route ran commuter streetcars along the southern boundary of both Margaret's and Bridget's tracts as well as along Telegraph Road. This route fronted the Montgomery, McCourtney, and Evoy families' properties and businesses. This improvement facilitated the marketing of individual lots in the McCourtney tract as well as the Evoy tract, the latter now owned by Mary J. Evoy (John's widow) and the Montgomerys. Bridget's forward-thinking advocacy for transportation through the area would continue to bear fruit for decades.

As part of this ongoing development process, the original Evoy, Montgomery and McCourtney tracts (totaling roughly 158 acres combined) were gradually subdivided and sold off in small residential and commercial lots. This process provided revenue streams for the family for decades and helped maintain their high economic and social status. At the time of her death in 1896, Margaret held properties in Alameda County, Sacramento County

(Sherman Island), Monterey County, and Contra Costa County (a portion of Rancho El Sobrante). Additionally, Margaret's estate included a thousand shares (valued at $698.58 in 1900) in the Tombstone Consolidated Gold and Silver Mining Company, Arizona, and shares in the Renton Coal Company of Seattle, Washington. After her passing, Margaret's financial empire was complex enough that it required three to four years to fully administer. By the time her estate was finally settled in 1900, the total appraised value of her real property holdings was $69,285.34 (a little more than $2.6 million in 2024 dollars). She left large bequests to various charities that she and her mother had traditionally supported. The daughter of an Irish immigrant farmer had indeed done well but had not forgotten those who suffered.

Bridget Miranda Evoy left a reputation as an ambitious and multifaceted businesswoman whose prescience and perseverance produced a legacy of hard-earned success. Whether pushing through physical or emotional adversity or transcending gender-based barriers, she embodied strength and broke glass ceilings almost reflexively, long before the term came into vogue. Her attitude and independence might have been appreciated by feminists of the era, but she was not an activist in feminism and did not contribute to the fledgling women's movements that emerged in the 1850s, seeking suffrage, employment opportunities, workplace regulations, and the like. Those trails would be blazed through the work of advocates such as Clarina Howard Nichols, Georgiana Bruce Kirby, Eliza Farnham, Mary Virginia Terhune, Charlotte Perkins Gilman, and Margaret Fuller.

Although strong-willed, and driven, Bridget also had an unexpected, lighter side. Somewhere within the pragmatic, hard-nosed businesswoman lived an idealist. He family described her as "imaginative and full of dreams of great things to happen in the future."[25] In their perception, she was an optimist and a dreamer, traits that served her well as she coped with the harsh realities of escaping the famine in Ireland and carving out a life on the frontiers of Missouri and California. The same optimism helped her perceive opportunity as she navigated the course of her consequential life.

While their feminist peers wrote and spoke publicly about the need to address inequalities for woman, Bridget, and her daughters Margaret and Ellen provided examples of how women could serve as potent forces in a society dominated by patriarchal attitudes, perceptions, and expectations. Their fierce independence, free-thinking spirit, and willingness to shed gender-based constraints certainly provided a role model for how women could attain economic and social freedoms. Through the course of her life, Bridget showed that, ultimately, each of us is capable of defining ourselves and pursuing self-determination.

Notes

Preface

1. In 2024 the State of California awarded more than $100 million designated for thirty-three tribal land projects. The funding will be used for ancestral land return, implementation of traditional ecological knowledge and Indigenous expertise, habitat restoration, climate and wildfire resilience projects, and more. Furthermore, in 2024 the Chumash Tribe obtained federal recognition for the Chumash National Marine Sanctuary, which encompasses 4,543 square miles of Central California's coastal and ocean waters, providing protection to significant natural, cultural, and historical resources while bringing new opportunities for research, community engagement, and education and outreach.

Acknowledgments

1. I note the passing of Dottie Smith, Shasta County historian, author, and college history instructor on October 27, 2022.

Chapter 1

1. Nicholas and Steckel, *Tall but Poor.*
2. Woodham-Smith, *Great Hunger.*
3. Brennan, *Family in Ireland.*
4. O'Hara, *Partners in Production?*
5. Welter, *Dimity Convictions.*
6. Raftery and Delaney, *Irish Nuns and Education.* The scoil chois claí provided a rudimentary primary education to children of "nonconforming" (Catholic and Presbyterian) faiths in Ireland.
7. Almquist, "Pre-famine Ireland."
8. Furlong, *Mighty Wave.*
9. Madden, *United Irishmen.*
10. Following some initial successes, particularly in County Wexford, the uprising was suppressed by government militia and yeomanry forces, reinforced by units of the British Army, with a civilian and combatant death toll estimated between ten thousand and fifty thousand.

11. McCullagh, *Tie That Blinds*. By 1841 two-thirds of the Irish population lived on the land, and 50 percent of the farms were less than five acres.

12. Maxwell, *Everyday Life in Nineteenth Century Ireland*; McCabe, *Begging, Charity, and Religion in Pre-Famine Ireland*.

13. Cogan, *All-American Girl*.

14. Conway, "Extension of the Poor Law to Ireland."

15. Conway, "Extension of the Poor Law to Ireland." Between 1820 and 1860, more than one-third of all immigrants to the United States originated from Ireland.

16. Wilde, *Ancient Legends, Mystic Charms, and Superstitions of Ireland*.

17. Land Patent Records, St. Louis Land Office, 1828. On January 1, 1828, James Evoy purchased 160 acres on Hancock Prairie, Callaway Co., Missouri (Township 47N/Range 7W/ SW quarter of Section 36).

18. Phelps et al., *Contemporary Biography of California's Representative Men*. See the biography of Zachariah Montgomery based on an interview with him.

19. Kraus, "Across the Western Sea."

20. Johnson, "Temescal Pioneer." This article is based on interviews with Jane E. Montgomery and James P. Montgomery.

21. US population census for 1830, Bonhomme Township, St. Louis County, Missouri. James Evoy is identified incorrectly as James Avoy.

22. Missouri Probate Records, St. Louis City and County, available through the Missouri Historical Society. James Evoy died on August 9, 1830, and his will was probated on August 18. The probate record lists Bridget Evoy, wife of James Evoy; witnesses were Benjamin Ellenwood and George Bruster.

23. Harper, *Influence of Jane Austen's Works on Societal Attitudes*.

24. Smith-Rosenberg, *Disorderly Conduct*.

25. The parcel was immediately across the road from St. Louis University. The location was fortuitous as, several years later (1836), the Jesuits established a Catholic parish and St. Xavier College Church at the university.

26. Purdy, *An Historical Analysis of the Economic Growth*; Lass, *Navigating the Missouri*; Tweet and National Waterways Study, *History of Transportation on the Upper Mississippi & Illinois Rivers*.

27. From the mid-1830s to the mid-1840s, St. Louis competed with the ports of New Orleans, Pittsburgh, and Louisville in terms of volume of commerce, occasionally surpassing one or more of those ports.

28. Marshall, "Geography of the Early Port of St. Louis."

29. Bridget's residence in St. Louis is listed in St. Louis City Directories for 1837, 1841, 1842, and 1848.

30. Keemle, *St. Louis Directory for the Years 1840–1*.

31. Charlene Sullivan, email communication to the author, 2003; *Santa Cruz Surf*, October 19, 1885.

32. Walsh, "Women's Place on the American Frontier."

33. Green, *Green's St. Louis Directory*.

34. Index of St. Louis Marriages, 1804–76, St. Louis Historical Society.

35. Green, *Green's St. Louis Directory* for 1845 lists John McCourtney as a machinist at Enos & McCortney–Engine Builders and Machinists [*sic*]. John H. McCortney is listed as living on the south side of Olive Street west of Twelfth Street.

36. Richard B. Mason to Brigadier General R. Jones, August 17, 1848, in "Official Report on the Gold Mines," Museum of the City of San Francisco, http://sfmuseum.org/hist6/masonrpt.html. It was William Tecumseh Sherman who persuaded his commander, Colonel Mason, to visit the goldfields himself to verify the tales of gold strikes.

37. Levy, *They Saw the Elephant.*

Chapter 2

1. Lewis, "Regional Ideas and Reality." "Great American Desert" was a term used in the nineteenth century to describe the part of North America situated east of the Rocky Mountains to approximately the 100th meridian. It can be traced to maps from Stephen H. Long's 1820 scientific expedition.

2. Upon leaving Missouri, the emigrants were leaving the United States, hence the term "emigrant" rather than "immigrant."

3. Bagley, *With Golden Visions Bright Before Them*, 55.

4. Read, "Women and Children on the Oregon-California Trail."

5. US Population Census, California, 1850. About 3,500 females and 115,000 males traveled overland to California in 1849.

6. Sacred Heart Church, Oakland, *The Story of Sacred Heart Church, Oakland.* The May 15, 1849, departure date for the Evoy/McCourtney family comes from Bridget Evoy, "Information Wanted," *Marysville Herald*, February 4, 1851, p. 3, col. 3.

7. Montgomery, Jane, "Incidents Relative to Mother's Trip Across the Plains in 1849, as She Recalled Them, March 14, 1947," John J. Montgomery collection, Santa Clara University Archives and Special Collections, Santa Clara, CA (hereafter SCU). Mary Ann McCourtney was born in 1844 and James Francis McCourtney on March 6, 1846, both in St. Louis, Missouri. James was three years of age when his family traveled to California. He was active there as an artist until his death on December 29, 1918. See Hughes, *Artists in California.*

8. Gordon, *Fire, Pestilence, and Death.*

9. Eventually, the Indian Territory would encompass the present states of Oklahoma, Kansas, Nebraska, and part of Iowa.

10. Utley, *Life Wild and Perilous*; Enzler, *Jim Bridger.*

11. Clemmer, "Tail of the Elephant."

12. Unruh, *Plains Across.* According to Unruh's research, about 90 percent of the emigrants killed by Indians met their fate west of South Pass, primarily along the Snake and Humboldt Rivers.

13. Clemmer, "Tail of the Elephant"; Heizer, *They Were Only Diggers.*

14. Clemmer, "Tail of the Elephant"

15. Read, "Women and Children on the Oregon-California Trail." 8.

16. Haun, "Woman's Trip Across the Plains in 1849," 9.

17. Haun, "Woman's Trip Across the Plains in 1849," 9.

18. Haun, "Woman's Trip Across the Plains in 1849." 9.

19. Read, "Women and Children on the Oregon-California Trail."

20. Greasewood Creek is located near the landmark known as Devil's Gate in south-central Wyoming.

21. Heiskell and Steel, *Forty-Niner from Tennessee.*

22. Hafen and Hafen, *Fremont's Fourth Expedition.*

23. Bruff was a leading member of the Washington City Company wagon train. The journals of Heiskell, Bruff, and Alonzo Delano would later become oft-cited primary accounts of the California Trail and California Gold Rush.

24. Denig and Ewers, *Five Indian Tribes of the Upper Missouri.*

25. Jane Montgomery "Incidents Relative to Mother's Trip Across the Plains," SCU.

26. The Crow occupied the area around the Yellowstone River and its tributaries, particularly the valleys of the Powder, Wind, and Bighorn Rivers in what is now Montana.

27. Denig and Ewers, *Five Indian Tribes of the Upper Missouri.*

28. Clark, "Crow and Cheyenne Women."

29. Bagley, *With Golden Visions Bright Before Them.*

30. Alexander, *Brigham Young and the Expansion of the Mormon Faith.*

31. Clemmer, "Tail of the Elephant."

32. Enzler, *Jim Bridger;* US Army Corps of Topographical Engineers, *Expedition to the Valley of the Great Salt Lake of Utah.*

33. US Army Corps of Topographical Engineers, *Expedition to the Valley of the Great Salt Lake of Utah,* 84.

34. Heiskell and Steel, *Forty-Niner from Tennessee,* journal entry for September 4, 1849, paraphrasing John McCourtney. Jane also recalled (paraphrased from interviews for a 1951 article): "Just beyond Fort Bridger, the widow Evoy led her party into Mormon Territory, now part of the great state of Utah. A 3-day stop was made at Salt Lake, to replenish supplies."

35. Johnson, "Temescal Pioneer."

36. Jane Montgomery, "Incidents Relative to Mother's Trip Across the Plains," SCU.

37. Jane Montgomery, "Incidents Relative to Mother's Trip Across the Plains," SCU.

Chapter 3

1. Solberg, "Sabbath on the Overland Trail."

2. Jane Montgomery "Incidents Relative to Mother's Trip Across the Plains," SCU.

3. Brown and Steel, *A Forty-Niner from Tennessee.* Apparently, it took approximately two weeks for Bridget's wagon train to get from Fort Bridger to the Salt

Lake settlement, they spent one week in Salt Lake, then another two weeks on the Salt Lake Cutoff to get back to the main California Trail (essentially taking up the month of August on their side trip to Salt Lake).

4. Clemmer, "Tail of the Elephant," 272.

5. Barnard J. Reid diary entry for September 9, 1849, in Reid and Gordon, *Overland to California with the Pioneer Line.*

6. Scott, "Peter Lassen."

7. Brown and Steel, *A Forty-Niner from Tennessee.*

8. Brown and Steel, *A Forty-Niner from Tennessee.* This cutoff later became known as the Applegate-Lassen Trail and is located at modern Imlay, thirty miles west of Winnemucca, Nevada. The phrase, "he takes the road to avoid the mountain" refers to the Lassen's Cutoff.

9. On the trail segment extending between Steeple Rock and Lassen's Cutoff (September 6 through September 26), the trains of Heiskell, Bruff, Swain, Middleton, and Lord moved at a pace that placed them between two and five days of travel of the Evoy/McCourtney train. Bruff's train was traveling about five days ahead of Heiskell's train between the Sweetwater River and Lassen's Cutoff. Hence, the Evoy/McCourtney train was bookended between these two wagon trains.

10. Reeve and Reeve, "From Tennessee to California in 1849." Rebecca Reeve and her brothers had departed Independence, Missouri, only five days before Bridget's group, and the two groups appear to have moved at a similar pace throughout the Overland Trail system leading to the trailhead for Lassen's Cutoff.

11. At the end of the 1849 emigration many travelers asserted that the real reason Lassen established the cutoff was to direct wagon trains toward his Rancho de Bosquejo and its trading post, located in the northern Sacramento Valley.

12. Levy, *They Saw the Elephant*, 73.

13. Read et al., *The Journals, Drawings, and Other Papers of J. Goldsborough Bruff.*

14. Layton, "Stalking Elephants in Nevada," 256; Sweeney, *Lassen Trail.*

15. Hardesty, "Archeology of the Donner Party Tragedy."

16. Persifor F. Smith was military governor of California and simultaneously commander of the Pacific Division of the US Army in 1849.

17. When corrected for inflation, $100,000 in 1849 currency would be worth approximately $4,153,224 in 2025. See the CPI Inflation Calculator at https://www.officialdata.org/us/inflation/1849?amount=100000.

18. The only significant sources of livestock within striking distance of the Northern and Central Sierras were privately owned at a few large ranches located in the Sacramento Valley: Sutter's Fort, William Johnson's Ranch at Wheatland, and the ranches of Peter J. Davis and Peter Lassen situated at the terminus of Lassen's Cutoff. Located farther afield were the ranches of Sutter's Hock Farm and to the north the ranches of John Bidwell or Nye & Foster's rancho.

19. Official Home of the Pit River Tribe, https://pitrivertribe.gov; Isenberg, *Mining California.* "Hewisedawi" translates to "those from on top." The Pit River Bands' territory spanned the Devil's Garden volcanic plateau along the North

Fork Pit River surrounding Goose Lake and the western slopes of the Warner Mountains in northeastern California.

20. Isenberg, *Mining California*; Lightfoot et al., *California Indians and Their Environment*. In "Notes on the Occupation of Foothill Nisenan," the archaeologist Norman Wilson reports:

> Hill and mountain Nisenan winter villages were located on ridges adjacent to streams or on flats along the rivers, often between the 1,000- and 2,000-foot level, out of the fog belt and with a southern exposure. During certain periods of the year, many families lived away from their main villages while they engaged in subsistence activities. Every part of their territory was within one- or two-days' journey from the winter village; thus, it was possible to have some winter movement to the valley floor or up into the mountains by small groups of hunters, families, or those who wanted to visit or trade.

21. Kroeber, *Ishi in Two Worlds*.

22. Layton, "From Pottage to Portage."

23. John H. Peoples hailed originally from Corpus Christi, Texas, and was former editor of the *Texas Star* newspaper there. He also published *The American Flag*, a newspaper out of Matamoros, Tamaulipas, Mexico, during the 1846–48 American conflict with Mexico. Peoples drowned along with several others when his boat capsized during a military survey expedition of Trinidad Bay, Humboldt County, California, on June 4, 1850.

24. The Warner Mountains, unnamed during the 1849 emigration, were later named in honor of Captain William H. Warner of the Army Corps of Topographical Engineers, who was killed by Indians in an ambush just to the north of Lassen Pass.

25. Holliday and Swain, *The World Rushed In*, 272, quoting Pratt's journal entry for October 15.

26. Rogers, *Bear Flag Lieutenant*.

27. Durham, *California's Geographic Names*. Lassen Pass is notable for its location at the convergence of two trails, the Applegate toward southern Oregon and the southerly continuation of the Lassen Trail, extending south from Goose Lake to Lassen's Ranch at modern-day Vina, Tehama County, California.

28. Jane Montgomery's subsequent recounting of this incident described it as occurring in eastern Utah. However, this is most likely in error. The circumstances involved, geographic considerations, and other details all suggest this incident most likely occurred somewhere in the current northern borderland region between Nevada and California.

29. Jane Montgomery, "Incidents Relative to Mother's Trip Across the Plains," SCU.

30. Montgomery, "Incidents Relative to Mother's Trip Across the Plains," SCU.

31. Howell et al., *1849 California Trail Diaries of Elijah Preston Howell*.

32. Holliday and Swain, *The World Rushed In*.

33. Reeve and Reeve, "From Tennessee to California in 1849."

34. The exact site of the attack on Warner's party is uncertain; however, Lieutenant Williamson's map places the location about four miles south of the Oregon border near Eightmile Creek.

35. Reeve and Reeve, "From Tennessee to California in 1849." Rebecca Reeve wrote that the killing of her brother Clayton was by a raiding party of Modocs. Modocs were known to occasionally venture into the territory of the Hewisedawi, their southern neighbors.

Chapter 4

1. Rucker diary entry for October 18, 1849, in "Message from the President."

2. Historians attempting to reconstruct the principal route of the Lassen Trail have determined that while making several trips up and down the trail, the government relief workers (Peoples, Tod, and others) established a new shortcut along the trail at the south end of "Big Valley," which ascended a rocky ridge out of the Pit River watershed. This alternate trail took an easterly diversion from the main route of travel in order to avoid the numerous river crossings and the difficult and deep gorge within the volcanic terrain of present-day Muck Valley, Lassen County, California. Upon exiting the southern terminus of the Pit River Valley, the trail exited the Modoc Plateau region and entered the northern Sierra Nevada range.

3. Kurtz, *Mountain Maidu and Pioneers.*

4. John H. Peoples to Major Rucker, October 24, 1849, in "Message from the President." This camp, located fourteen miles north of the southern end of the Pit River Valley, served as a temporary base of operations for the government train as they waited for the remaining wagons and packers to arrive between October 22 and October 26, 1849.

5. "Message from the President."

6. This group included the large St. Louis Company train, which included General John Wilson, the newly appointed navy agent and principal Indian agent for Alta California. Recall that General Wilson's large train had entered the Mormon settlement at Salt Lake at about the same time as the Evoy/McCourtney group in late August, 1949.

7. "Message from the President."

8. John K. Root had been a member of the Wolverine Rangers Company and had chosen to separate from the group to become a packer somewhere along the Humboldt River in central Nevada.

9. This reunion would have occurred somewhere between the Pit River Valley and the more southerly Feather River Valley.

10. John K. Root to "Government Relief Company," October 28, 1849, in "Message from the President."

11. John H. Peoples to Major Rucker, December 12, 1849, in "Message from the President."

12. Bruff, journal entry for October 27, 1849, in Bruff et al., *Gold Rush.*

13. Kroeber, *Ishi in Two Worlds*, 39.

14. Sapir and Spier, *Notes on the Culture of the Yana.*

15. Angulo, *Indians in Overalls.*

16. Jane Montgomery, "Incidents Relative to Mother's Trip Across the Plains," SCU.

17. Bruff, journal entry for November 3, 1849, in Bruff et al., *Gold Rush*, 228.

18. Peoples to Major Rucker, December 12, 1849, in "Message from the President."

19. William Swain, diary entry for November 6, 1849, in "Message from the President."

20. Holliday and Swain, *World Rushed In*, 286.

21. Holliday and Swain, *World Rushed In*, 288.

22. Reeve and Reeve, "From Tennessee to California in 1849," 49.

23. The Narrows is located at 40°9.888′ N, 121 40.566′ W, on Forest Service Road 27N08, near Butte Meadows, Tehama County, California.

24. Peoples to Elisha H. Todd, November 12, 1849, in "Message from the President."

25. Peoples to Elisha H. Todd, November 12, 1849, in "Message from the President."

26. Bruff, journal entry for November 12, 1849, in Bruff et al., *Gold Rush.*

27. Peter J. Davis (1798–1873) was one of the original explorers of Lassen's Cutoff (along with Peter Lassen) in 1848, and in October of that year settled at Feather River (Yuba County), where he embarked in placer mining operations. Davis remained on the Feather River until June 1850, then relocated to the settlement of Santa Clara in Santa Clara County, where he engaged in stock-raising and farming.

28. Major D. H. Rucker to Major General P. F. Smith, December 20, 1849, in "Message from the President."

Chapter 5

1. John Sutter, "Derivation of Our County Name," letter to the editor, *Marysville Herald*, September 3, 1850. Sutter named the Yuba River in 1840 for a village of Indigenous people who identified themselves as the "Yubu" located opposite the confluence of the Yuba and Feather Rivers. Yuba County and Yuba City were anglicized from the tribal name.

2. Keim, *Society in Washington*, based in part on an interview with Ellen Evoy Montgomery.

3. Bates, *Incidents on Land and Water.*

4. Stephen J. Field served on the California Supreme Court (1857–63), then was appointed as a US Supreme Court justice (1863–97).

5. Field, *Personal Reminiscences of Early Days in California*, 26.

6. Ramey, "Beginnings of Marysville: Part I."

7. Twain, *Roughing It.*

8. Map of Yuba City, 1849, Situated at the Head of Navigation on the Feather River opposite the Mouth of Yuba River as Surveyed by Jos. S. Ruth," Deed Book E, p. 63, Office of the County Clerk, Sutter County, Yuba City, CA.

9. The 1850 censes (taken in November) records two adult laborers (presumable boarders or tenants) residing at Bridget's Marysville residence.

10. Deed Book B, March 20, 1850, p. 89, Office of the County Clerk, Sutter County. These purchases totaled approximately $16,025, corrected for inflation in 2024 dollars. (CPI Inflation Calculator, https://www.officialdata.org).

11. Delay, *History of Yuba and Sutter Counties.*

12. When corrected for inflation to 2024 dollars, $400 in 1850 dollars is equal to $16,353.04 (CPI Inflation Calculator, https://www.officialdata.org). This parcel was located on the southeast corner of the intersection of Fremont Street and Lafayette Street. Peter J. Davis had recently relocated to Santa Clara, and Bridget's previous acquaintanceship with him no doubt facilitated the land purchase.

13. CPI Inflation Calculator, https://www.officialdata.org/.

14. Isenberg, *Mining California.*

15. Tiemann, "Discounting Gold: Money and Banking in California," Global History of Capitalism Project, case study 22, Oxford Centre for Global History, April 2021, https://globalcapitalism.history.ox.ac.uk/files/goldrushbankingcasepdf.

16. Mann, *After the Gold Rush*; Whitney, *Auriferous Gravels of the Sierra Nevada.*

17. *Sacramento Daily Union*, March 15, 1852, p. 2. The reported cost of bridge construction was $8,000 ($327,060.78 in 2024 dollars). It is unknown what share of the cost was fronted by Van Court versus the McCourtneys.

18. Davis, *Illustrated History of Sacramento County*; Chamberlain and Wells, *History of Yuba County.*

19. Isenberg, *Mining California*, 20.

20. Royce, *Frontier Lady.*

21. Wilson and Wright, *Luzena Stanley Wilson, '49er*, 23.

22. Isenberg, *Mining California.*

23. Zach Montgomery, "Personal Remembrances: Sacramento City in 1850," *Family's Defender Magazine and Educational Review* 4 (1884): 119–28, Bancroft Library, University of California–Berkeley (hereafter BL).

24. In 1849 Sarah Royce observed that only a handful of women were residing in the various settlements situated within a day's travel of Weaverville in (soon to be) El Dorado County.

25. In fact, when a formal dance was proposed at Marysville's Covillaud Hotel, considerable pressure was made to induce the women in the settlement to participate. When the ball commenced, seven women attended, hardly enough to form two dancing sets.

26. Levy, *They Saw the Elephant.*

27. Noy, *Gold Rush Stories*, 152.

28. Davis, *Illustrated History of Sacramento County.*

29. According to family oral tradition, Bridget and Ellen ran a boardinghouse for miners in a community called Bear Valley. The family seems to have confused

them with Margaret, who ran a hotel/eatery (at least as late as April 1863) at McCourtney's Crossing at the Bear River Canyon in Yuba County. Later, Bridget and Ellen did establish the California House at Briggsville, Shasta County.

30. Wheatland Historical Society, *Wheatland.*

31. Spearman, *John Joseph Montgomery.*

32. Bates, *Incidents on Land and Water.*

33. Hurtado, "Indians in Town and Country."

34. Norman Wilson, "Notes on the Occupation of Foothill Nisenan at Contact Times in the Auburn-Lincoln Area, Placer County," 1994, unpublished manuscript on file with the author.

35. Heizer, *They Were Only Diggers.*

36. Recognizing the actions against Native peoples since California statehood, in 2019, the Governor of California's office issued a formal apology to California's Native Americans for "historical mistreatment, violence, and neglect." This executive order also established a Truth and Healing Council (THC) to "provide Native Americans a platform to clarify the historical record and work collaboratively with the state to begin the healing process." Executive Order N-15-19, https://www.gov.ca.gov/wp-content/uploads/2019/06/6.18.19-Executive -Order.pdf.

37. Wilkerson et al., *Roadside Geology and Mining History of the Mother Lode.* Extracting the quartz (a very hard mineral) from the host rock was highly labor intensive. The material had to be mechanically separated by breaking down the host rock into blocks and crushing it to isolate the gold-bearing quartz from the detritus.

38. US Population Census, 1850: Yuba City and Vicinity, Sutter, California, roll 36, p. 55a.

39. Jane Montgomery, "Incidents Relative to Mother's Trip Across the Plains," SCU; Ellen Evoy Montgomery interview in Phelps et al., *Contemporary Biography of California's Representative Men.*

40. Faye, "Notes on the Southern Maidu." Longs Bar (or Long Bar) was located fourteen miles east of Marysville along a route to the quartz-mining operations at the settlement of Nevada, California Territory.

41. Jane Montgomery, "Incidents Relative to Mother's Trip Across the Plains," SCU.

42. Shuck, *History of the Bench and Bar of California.* Hastings later founded Hastings College of Law at San Francisco.

43. Lewis Publishing Co., *A Memorial and Biographical History of Northern California.* Fowler also served briefly as an alcalde of Sacramento City and member of the Board of Commissioners that framed the code of laws for the district.

44. Madley, *American Genocide.*

45. Isenberg, *Mining California.*

46. *S. C. Hastings et al., vs. John S. Fowler,* Case No. 853, Sixth District Court, Sacramento District, reported in the *Sacramento Daily Union,* February 26, 1852, p. 4. On December 15, 1851, McCourtney et al. won a judgment of $7,552 with interest, which was apparently Fowler's obligation in the unpaid mortgage.

Fowler's property in Sacramento was put up for sale to pay the plaintiffs by order of a writ of execution.

47. Population Schedules of the Seventh Census of the United States, 1850, Yuba City & Vicinity, Sutter County, Enumeration District, enumerated November 5, 1850.

48. US Geological Survey, *Tertiary Gold-Bearing Channel Gravel.*

49. Mann, *After the Gold Rush.*

50. Isenberg, *Mining California.*

51. In more advanced mining operations, inclined secondary tunnels were excavated and surface water was directed to flow into the tunnels so that excavated alluvial and bedrock materials could be washed and removed with buckets or ore carts.

52. Isenberg, *Mining California*

53. As early as 1849, a particularly rich placer lead had been discovered in the vicinity of Wet Hill, in the northeastern portion of the mining settlement of Nevada, California Territory.

54. *Sacramento Daily Union,* September 26, 1851; see also *Nevada Journal,* September 25, 1851, and *Daily Alta California,* September 28, 1851. Myers may have been the W. E. Myers listed as a miner at Oriental Mill along Deer Creek in Bean, *Bean's History and Directory of Nevada County, California.* Evidence of John McCourtney's gold-mining activity also comes from Margaret P. McCourtney's obituary in the *San Francisco Chronicle* on August 19, 1896, which was probably penned by her daughter: "Mrs. Margaret McCourtney, with her husband and children came to California in the days of the rush for gold. Her husband mined in Yuba County for several years and was quite fortunate for he had accumulated considerable wealth."

55. Bancroft, *California Inter Pocula.* The bylaws pertaining to the Myers Ravine Mining District were originally published in the *Nevada Journal,* January 27, 1854. This placer mining district consisted of approximately one hundred square feet of hillside/sluice mining bordering the north side of the larger Wet Hill Mining District.

56. Khan, "Married Women's Property Laws," 358. On April 12, 1852, the California Legislature approved "An Act to authorize married women to transact business in their own name as sole traders."

57. Haynes, "Map of the County of Alameda"; Wagner et al., *"Map Showing Portions of Alameda and Contra Costa Counties."*

Chapter 6

1. Webb, *Centenary of Catholicity in Kentucky.* Zach Montgomery's personal copy of the book containing his marginal notations are in the author's personal collection.

2. For biographies of Zach Montgomery, see Baker, *Past and Present of Alameda County;* Bancroft, *History of the Pacific States,* vol. 7; Delay, *History of Yuba and Sutter Counties; History of the State of California and Biographical Record of Oakland;*

Herringshaw, *Herringshaw's Encyclopedia of American Biography*; Phelps et al., *Contemporary Biography of California's Representative Men*; Shanahan, "Zachariah Montgomery"; Shuck, *History of the Bench and Bar of California*; Thompson & West, *Official and Historical Atlas of Alameda County*; Chamberlain, *History of Sutter County*.

3. Bidwell, *Journal of a Trip to California in 1841*. Major John Bidwell (1819–1900) was an early pioneer in California. He attained the rank of major during the US War with Mexico (1848), served as a member of the California Senate from the Sacramento District (1849–51), presided over the first (1850) and third (1860) California state censuses, and was promoted to brigadier general during the Civil War (1863). He served as a US congressman (1865–67), and was a candidate for US president in 1892. A prominent rancher in Northern California in what is now Chico ("Rancho Chico"), he grew vegetables and raised livestock on a large scale.

4. Zach Montgomery, "Personal Reminiscences: First Thoughts of California," *Family's Defender Magazine and Educational Review* 3 (1883): 260-61, BL. John Bidwell would later call on Zach in Washington, DC, in 1887 when Zach was serving as US assistant attorney general in the Department of the Interior during the first administration of Grover Cleveland. See John Bidwell, journal entries for February 26, 1887, and March 7, 1887, Bidwell Papers, California State Library, Sacramento (hereafter CSL).

5. Montgomery, "Personal Reminiscences: First Thoughts."

6. Zach Montgomery, "Address Delivered Before the Erodelphian Society, St. Joseph's College, on the Anniversary of the College, April 19, 1849," Department of Archives and Special Collections, Fordham University, New York, NY.

7. Zach Montgomery, "Personal Reminiscences: First Thoughts." Among the emigrant company that Zach traveled with was Thomas E. Hayden, future senator from Nevada and US Attorney for the Nevada District.

8. Stagnero, "Kentuckian Views Gold-Mad Sacramento," quoting interviews with Jane E. and James P. Montgomery given in 1953 and 1954.

9. Phelps et al., *Contemporary Biography of California's Representative Men*, 69.

10. Zach Montgomery, "Personal Reminiscences: Sacramento City in 1850—The Squatter Fight—Frightful Revenges of Cholera in the Infant City," *Family's Defender Magazine and Educational Review* 3 (1884): 239–46, BL.

11. In 1850, Ringgold was a small mining camp and trading post located in a narrow valley alongside Weber Creek, two miles southwest of Placerville, El Dorado County, California. "El Dorado" is Spanish for "The Gilded One."

12. Zach Montgomery, "Personal Reminiscences: Sacramento City in 1850." Emphasis original.

13. Zach Montgomery, "Personal Reminiscences: Sacramento City in 1850."

14. Tyson, Derby, et al., *Geology and Industrial Resources of California*.

15. Tyson, Smith, et al., *Report of the Secretary of War*.

16. Zach Montgomery, "Personal Reminiscences: First Thoughts," 261.

17. Montgomery, "Personal Reminiscences: Sacramento City in 1850."

18. Chamberlain and Wells, *History of Yuba County California*. Hansonville was established in 1851 by James H. Hanson.

19. Phelps et al., *Contemporary Biography of California's Representative Men.*

20. For the naming of Montgomery Creek after Zach, see Steger and Jones, *Place Names of Shasta County.* Also Smith, "Covered Wagon," 1991, pp 49–62; Dottie Smith, Shasta County historian, email to Craig S, Harwood, 2002. In July 2024 the Shasta Land Trust working with Pacific Gas & Electric Company established the 1,612-acre Burney Gardens Conservation District in eastern Shasta County. This land is returned to stewardship of the Pit River Tribe. The Burney Gardens area is the ancestral territory of the Atsugewi Band of the Pit River peoples.

21. California State Parks, "Shasta State Historic Park," https://www.parks.ca.gov/pages/456/files/ShastaSHPFinalWebLayout050917.pdf. An article in the *Marysville Daily Appeal,* June 4, 1885, discusses Zach's early history as an attorney in Shasta City and a farmer in Shasta County.

22. Shanahan, "Zachariah Montgomery"; Shuck, *History of the Bench and Bar of California;* Weber, *Catholic Footprints in California;* Weber, *Readings in California Catholic History.*

23. Herringshaw, *Herringshaw's Encyclopedia of American Biography;* *New York Times,* May 26, 1885, p. 3; *New York Times,* May 29, 1885, p. 1.

Chapter 7

1. "Bridges on Bear River," *Sacramento Daily Union,* March 15, 1852, p. 2.

2. Clear Creek, a tributary of the Sacramento River in the southern Klamath Mountain Range in Shasta County, contained extensive placer deposits and was first explored shortly after the 1848 gold discovery at Sutter's Mill.

3. Vaughan et al., *Gold and Lumber.*

4. Giles, *Shasta County,* 53.

5. Hubert Bancroft, in volume 6 of *History of California,* reported Briggsville to be a "prominent camp near Clear Creek [Shasta County] supplied by a ditch from Cottonwood Creek," 366.

6. United States Population Census, State of California, 1852, lists the surname "Evoy" on two pages within the Clear Creek enumeration district. On p. 3 Bridget and Ellen are identified as merchants (both recorded as females but their ages incorrectly listed as 46 and 22, respectively). Another census entry, "Schedule I" (p. 27) lists M. E. Evoy (female of 37 years) operating a boarding-house and a William Evoy (24 years) identified as a miner.

7. The *Shasta Courier,* March 25, 1854, contains an advertisement signed by B. M. Evoy announcing the availability of the California House for sale.

8. "Correspondence from Shasta," *Pacific* (San Francisco, CA), June 18, 1852.

9. Mary Ballou to Selden Ballou, 1852, in Ballou, "*'I Hear the Hogs in My Kitchen.'*" The placer mining settlement of Negro Bar was named to recognize the African American gold miners who discovered gold there in 1849. It was later established as a Sacramento County park and, in 2022, was renamed Black Miners Bar by the California State Parks and Recreation Commission.

10. Ballou, "*'I Hear the Hogs in My Kitchen.'*"

11. William Swain to George Swain, January 6, 1850, in Holliday and Swain, *The World Rushed In*, 319.

12. Smith, *Dictionary of Early Shasta County History*; Evoy, B. M., mortgagee, to Lean, mortgager, Mortgage Book C. p. 296, Shasta County Historical Society; *Shasta Courier*, August 18, 1855. About seven months later "Mr. Lean's Hotel" is noted in the *Shasta Courier*, December 1, 1855, p. 2. In August 1861 Lean's Hotel in Briggsville ("The Commercial Hotel") was advertised for sale.

13. J. A. Ruff, "Letter from Briggsville," *Shasta Courier*, May 28, 1853, p. 1; Wells et al., *History of Butte County*; *Sacramento Daily Union*, December 31, 1853, p. 2. Note that $1,800 in 1853 money would be worth nearly $73,588.68, when corrected for inflation to 2024.

14. Leek, *John Bidwell*; Bidwell, Gillis, and Magliari, *John Bidwell and California*; Bidwell, Quaife, and Steele, *Echoes of the Past About California*.

15. California State Senate, "Record of State Senators, 1849–2021," https://archive.senate.ca.gov/sites/archive.senate.ca.gov/files/senators_and_officers_1849_2021.pdf. Harper was one of the men wounded in the Squatters' Riot at Sacramento in August 1850.

16. Dry Creek House was reportedly located about ten miles past Samuel Neal's Ranch ("Rancho Esquon"), near present-day Durham, Butte County, California.

17. "District Court," *Weekly Butte Record, December 31, 1853.*

18. "Further News from California," *Miners Express*, July 12, 1853; *Sacramento Daily Union*, May 30, 1853.

19. "Grave Accusation," *Shasta Courier*, May 28, 1853.

20. "District Court," *Weekly Butte Record*, December 31, 1853.

21. "Col. Harper," *Shasta Courier*, June 4, 1853.

22. "District Court," *Weekly Butte Record*, December 31, 1853.

23. "Colonel Harper," *Shasta Courier*, January 7, 1854.

24. *New York Times*, June 25, 1853.

25. California State Legislature, *Journal of the House*, 84.

26. *Chico Weekly Chronicle*, December 31, 1853; *Shasta Courier*, December 29, 1855.

27. Wells et al., *History of Butte County*, 179.

28. Osborne, *J. Granville Doll*. William Myers was a pioneer who helped establish the community of Red Bluff (or Red Bluffs), Tehama County, California.

29. The Bidwell family estate had been established the previous year (1852). Rancho Chico became famous throughout the West for its extensive gardens filled with plants from all over the world. The Marysville–Shasta Road connected Marysville with the mining settlements in southern Shasta County, including Clear Creek.

30. Bridget M. Evoy to John Bidwell, June 13, 1853, Bidwell Papers, CSL.

31. William Myers to John Bidwell, July 5, 1853, CSL. On this date Mr. Myers wrote to Bidwell stating, "I Rec'd your note this morning stating that I could not Rec' [receive] any more vegetables on account of the unwillingness of the drivers to take them aboard."

32. Bancroft, *The Works of Hubert Howe Bancroft: History of California*, 4:385.

33. Bancroft, *History of California*, 4:385.

34. Miller, *Joaquin Miller's Romantic Life*, 53.

35. *Shasta Courier*, August 27, 1853.

36. *Shasta Courier*, October 1, 1853.

37. *Shasta Courier*, September 24, 1853.

38. Francis L. Aude, "Personal History of Zach Montgomery," letter collected prior to 1879 and referenced for the compilation *History of Yuba County* by Thompson & West (1879), Microfilm TW 135-TW 106, Yuba County Public Library, Yuba City, CA (hereafter YCPL). See also Colville, *Colville's Marysville Directory*. The directory lists Z. Montgomery Attorney at Law. Law office located on D Street, between Second and Third, with a residence in Yuba City.

39. "California Marriages and Deaths," *New York Times*, August 8, 1854. The article states, "In Marysville, July 4, Zachariah Montgomery of Marysville Bar, formerly of Kentucky and recently of Shasta, and Miss Helena Graham, of Marysville."

Chapter 8

1. Contra Costa (Spanish for "opposite coast") was so named because of its location across the bay from San Francisco. "Alameda" was a common Spanish word for a grove of poplar trees or a tree-shaded promenade.

2. City of Berkeley, "Cultural Resources Technical Report."

3. Halley, *Centennial Year Book of Alameda County*, 443.

4. Norman, *Temescal Legacies*. The village of Temescal was centered around the modern intersection of Telegraph Avenue and Clairmont Boulevard in North Oakland. It is surmised that the Peraltas, or perhaps one of their ranch's vaqueros, had seen local Indigenous Ohlone structures along the nearby creek similar to those in other parts of New Spain that the Spanish knew as *temescalli*. "Temescal," derived from the Nahuatl language of the Mexica (Aztec) people of Mexico, means "sweat house."

5. Gudde, *California Place Names*; Mike Racoon Eyes Kinney, "The Prehistoric Huchiun Band of the Native Ohlone at Garrity Creek & Along San Pablo Bay," August 7, 2014, San Francisco Bay Area Indymedia, https://www.indybay.org/newsitems/2014/08/07/18759733.php; Milliken, *Time of Little Choice*; Milliken et al., *Ohlone/Costanoan Indians of the San Francisco Peninsula*. The word "Huchiun" simply means "people." The Huchiun band of the Ohlone people occupied western Contra Costa County and the future metropolitan areas of Oakland, Berkeley, and Richmond. Living in groups of 250 or fewer people, they maintained seasonal villages in the area and practiced a hunting-and-gathering lifestyle.

6. Hague and Langum, *Thomas O. Larkin*.

7. *Ambro, "Spanish Colonial Era."* So prolific was the scavenging by grizzlies that don Vicente Peralta and his vaqueros engaged the bears for sport, an extremely dangerous sport. They rode through the slaughtering pens, chasing, lassoing, momentarily restraining, or sometimes capturing or killing bears.

8. Davis, *Sixty Years in California*, 100.

9. *Ambro, "Spanish Colonial Era"*; Haynes and Haynes, *Grizzly Bear*.

10. Wollenberg, *Berkeley: A City in History*.

11. Clay, "Property Rights and Institutions."

12. Isenberg, *Mining California*.

13. Adams, *Oakland's Early History*, 16. Horace Carpentier changed the name from Contra Costa to Oakland in his request for township incorporation, and the bill was passed on May 4, 1852.

14. San Pablo Historical and Museum Society, "San Pablo History: Our Forgotten Pioneers," September 4, 2021, https://sites.google.com/sanpablohistoricalsociety .com/museums/san-pablo-history?authuser=0.

15. Deed Book A, December 9, 1853, Office of the Alameda County Clerk, Oakland, CA (hereafter ALCC). The deed records the land as consisting of "about 97 acres situated in the town of Contra Costa, County of Alameda." This parcel was designated as Tract No. 36 on the tract map of Julius Kellersberger, "Map of the Vicente & Domingo Peralta Ranchos." Farming equipment that came with the property purchase included "agricultural implements including two ploughs, one harrow, hoes and shovel, scythe, rakes and pitching forks, baskets with a lot of loose pickets (Redwood)."

16. Bowman, J. N. "Birthdays of Urban Communities"; Verbarg, *Celebrities at Your Doorstep*, contains biographical information on John J. Montgomery, his siblings, parents, and grandmother Bridget Evoy.

17. *Evoy v. Tewksbury*, 5 Cal. 285 (Cal. 1855). *Sacramento Daily Union*, July 11, 1855. McMakin would later be convicted of arson in 1857 and of assault with a deadly weapon in 1859 in San Francisco.

18. B. M. Evoy, "The California House for Sale," *Shasta Courier*, March 25, 1854.

19. "Cotillion Party," *Shasta Courier*, August 18, 1854.

20. Deed, John Parks to Ellen Evoy, 1853, Book of Deeds, Office of the County Clerk of Sutter County, Yuba City, CA; also, Yuba County Grantee Index for 1853.

21. "Oakland and Her Improvements."

22. J. P. Montgomery to Windsor Josselyn, March 16, 1947, SCU.

23. The University of California–Berkeley, located just north of the former Peralta homestead, adopted the grizzly (golden bear) as their sports mascot in 1895. In 1911 the California Golden Bear flag was adopted.

24. Early tax assessments for Yuba County (1863–64) identified Margaret McCourtney as the sole proprietor of the hotel/eatery and general store at McCourtney's Crossing.

25. The 1860 census for East Bear River Township indicates a forty-year-old miner named Peter Myers and two laborers (an Englishman, John McFalls, and a German, William Myers) were living at the crossing, in addition to the two Indian teenagers and a Chinese man, Ah Hua, identified as a servant. The laborers were most likely hired hands who worked on the ranch.

26. *Sacramento Daily Union*, May 12, 1862.

27. Mikesell, "Suspension Bridges of Andrew Smith Hallidie."

28. Sayenga, *"Contextual Essay on Wire Bridges."* In this role, Hallidie made important contributions to the transportation history of the Sierran mother

lode, designing bridges that were robust enough to withstand the numerous floods that inundated the region during the early 1860s.

29. *Marysville Daily Appeal*, May 1, 1863, and June 30, 1863.

30. *Engineering and Mining Journal*. Over time these copper deposits became recognized as part of a 180-mile-long belt (the Sierra Foothill Copper Belt) extending from the area of Marysville to as far south as Fresno.

Chapter 9

1. The bond states that firm of Bayerque & Pinoche (of San Francisco) provided a bond for a property deed equal to $10,000.00 on behalf of Mrs. Bridget M. Evoy. Alameda County Hall of Records, Deed Book G, October 6, 1857, pp. 105–6, ALCC. In the following year (1858) Bridget repaid the loan. On August 28, 1858, Bridget M. Evoy paid $3,250.00 to Francis Alfred L. Pinoche for Tract No. 36 "located on the west side of "Peralta Road'" (Alameda County Hall of Records, Deeds Book H, pp. 279–80, ALCC).

2. Alameda County Hall of Records, 1858 Deeds, August 27, 1858, ALCC, deed from James Hepburn and others to Margaret P. McCourtney. Margaret purchased the land for $1,901.25 from James Hepburn and his business partner Evelyn R. Faulker, both prominent San Francisco merchants.

3. On December 17, 1861, Bridget sold her San Francisco property on Vallejo Street in the Russian Hill district to Margaret McCourtney, who leased a portion of that land to her sister Mary Ann Mullikin. See California Supreme Court et al., *Reports of Cases Determined*.

4. Township 1 of Contra Costa County includes the area occupied by the present-day community of Greenbriar. El Sobrante Ranch was granted to Juan José and Victor Castro by the Mexican nation on April 22, 1841. Many of the early settlers in San Pablo were Catholic, and in 1864, St. Paul's Church (in San Pablo, California) was built on land donated by the Alvarado/Castro family.

5. In January 1860, John Evoy and Joseph D. Mullikin were sued by Augustus Schenk and Adolphus Schwartz in the California Supreme Court over title to the land they were occupying at Cruzito Valley. This suit carried on for several years but was eventually decided in favor of the defendants, Mullikin and Evoy.

6. US Population Census, 1860, Contra Costa County, Martinez & San Pablo Township, June 12, p. 5. John Evoy had a hired laborer, William Gilchrist, living at the ranch to help with maintenance.

7. Records, Sutter County Office of the District Attorney, Yuba City, California; Chamberlain, *History of Sutter County*.

8. Death notice for Helena Frances Montgomery, *Marysville Herald*, July 20, 1856. The St. Joseph's Cemetery, Marysville, Internment Register indicates Helean Francis Montgomery was born December 20, 1835, at Rochester, New York, and died July 18, 1856, at Yuba City.

9. Baker, *Past and Present of Alameda County*; Phelps et al., *Contemporary Biography of California's Representative Men*.

10. US Population Census for 1860, Sutter County, Yuba Township, roll 70, p. 770. The census lists Zach's law office at 61 D Street, Marysville, CA.

11. Birth announcement for twins John and Zachariah Montgomery, *Daily Alta California*, February 17, 1858; the birth was also announced in the *Marysville Daily Appeal*, February 28, 1858.

12. Birth announcement for Margaret Helena and Ellen Rose, born on February 24, 1861, in *Marysville Daily National Democrat*, February 27, 1861.

13. Deed Book F, April 22, 1860, pp. 337–38, Sutter County Recorder's Office. Bridget and Zach jointly purchased a portion of Lot 4, Block 2 from George M. Hanson for one dollar.

14. Deed Book G, January 5, 1866, pp. 589–90, Sutter County Recorder's Office, Yuba City. The downtown Yuba City lot was sold to a local named John Kuper for $150 in gold coin.

15. California Secretary of State, *California Blue Book* (State Roster), 1907, p. 606; Shanahan, "Zachariah Montgomery"; Ramey, "Election of 1860 in Sutter and Yuba Counties," contains a brief biography of Zach.

16. Wheat, "California's Bantam Cock." Several entries from DeLong's journal describe Zach. On July 28, 1858, he wrote: "Montgomery opened the case after the recess and spoke loud, long and most terribly—gave me particular hell." His journal entry for July 5, 1858 stated "Zach Montgomery followed the previous speakers with a howl." A newspaper correspondent from the *National Daily Democrat* who witnessed another exchange between Zach and Colonel Ed Baker stated, "Zach Montgomery, the fiery Lecomptonite followed with a short harangue and Colonel Baker peppered ol' Zach with a considerable quantity of hot shot, after which, Zach returned to the charge . . . all in all, it must have been a grand evening for the admirers of oratory" (*National Daily Democrat*, July 7, 1859). Another journal entry of Charles DeLong (August 4, 1859) states, "I challenged Montgomery, who opened with a flaming speech and I followed, about fifteen ladies were on the balcony, and the boys cheered and fired anvils lustily."

17. Zach Montgomery, "State of the Union," February 11, 1861, SCU.

18. Zach and Ellen's children were, in birth order: John Joseph Montgomery (1858–1911), Zachariah Montgomery Jr. (1858–61), Mary Clotilda Montgomery (1859–1949), Margaret Helena Montgomery (1861–1931), Ellen Rose Montgomery (1861–64), Richard Joseph Montgomery (1863–1932), James Patrick Montgomery (1865–1956), and Jane Elizabeth Montgomery (1869–1955).

19. Quoted in Dare, "Prof. J. J. Montgomery—The Personality of the Man," *San Francisco Call*, May 7, 1905.

20. Hyman, "New Light on *Cohen v. Wright*."

21. Chandler, "California's 1863 Loyalty Oaths."

22. *Marysville Daily Democrat Appeal*, February 14, 1861. This lengthy article discusses Zach's speeches regarding the Lincoln administration.

23. The Interment Register for St. Joseph's Catholic Cemetery, Marysville, lists the following internment information for the surname Montgomery: Helena Frances Montgomery (Zach's first wife) born December 20, 1835 (Rochester, NY), died July 18, 1856. Thomas Montgomery, born 1856, died December 28, 1861, 6 years and 15 days old. Zachariah Montgomery, died December 28, 1861 at 9:00 pm at 3 years, 10 months, and 13 days old. Ellen Rose Montgomery, born February 23, 1861, died March 6, 1864, at 3 years, 11 days old.

24. Zachariah Montgomery, early 1884, handwritten, three-page first draft of a manuscript and typed pages of the same manuscript recounting family history and the origin of the surname Montgomery, in the author's personal collection. In April 1864 Bridget Evoy sold twenty-three acres of her land on Telegraph Road (between Rose Garland Way and 43rd St.) to Zach and Ellen for $1,000 on the condition that she would be allowed to maintain a home on the property (this deed gift would later become the subject of a California Supreme Court case).

25. Zach and Ellen would later build a large home adjacent to Bridget's original residence in 1868. This home was destroyed by fire in August 1888. See "A Fierce Fire: The Old Residence of Zach Montgomery Burned Today," *Oakland Enquirer*, August 27, 1888.

26. Montgomery, *Poison Fountain*; Peden, Pacific Coast History of Education Society, *Opposition to Public Education in California*. Believing firmly that parents should have rights to direct their children's education and should determine how tax revenues should be spent for education, in 1861 Zach authored the Montgomery Bill (Assembly Bill 348) for educational reform. The Montgomery Bill marked the beginning of Zach's advocacy for the revision of the state's compulsory public education system, a cause he pursued for the remainder of his life.

27. Zach Montgomery open letter to Major-General McDowell published as a pamphlet, 1865, BL,

28. Twain, "Democratic Meeting at Hayes Park," *San Francisco Morning Call*, August 3, 1864.

29. Guinn, *History of the State of California*; Tinkham, *California and the Civil War*.

30. *Daily Alta California*, April 16, 1865.

31. Hal Johnson, who wrote a column describing Oakland history, published a series of lengthy articles concerning the history of the Montgomery and Evoy families, based on interviews with Jane E. Montgomery and James P. Montgomery. See Johnson, "So We Are Told," *Berkeley Daily Gazette*, December 19, 20, 24, and 26, 1951.

32. In fact, Lincoln had been shot while seated in his cherished rocker at the Lincoln Theatre and, after his assassination, the bloodstained chair served as a touchstone of the tragedy and a focus of public sympathy within American popular culture as the "Lincoln Rocker." Bridget's circa late 1850s Rococo Revival rocking chair has been passed down through five generations of descendants and is in the author's possession.

Chapter 10

1. US Population Census, Schedule L, 1860, Oakland Township, Alameda County, California.

2. King and Dingee, "Map of Oakland, Berkeley, and Alameda"; Hettich, "Checking Up on the Montgomery Family," *San Ysidro Border Press*, May 20, 1950. Stilwell, *Directory of the Township and City of Oakland*, lists Zach's residence as being located between Rose Garland Way and Ellen Street, Oakland Township.

Rosegarland Way was later renamed Evoy Street and, in 1870, was brought into conformance with the city street system as 40th Street. Ellen Street became 42nd Street.

3. Jane Montgomery, "A Few Notes and Anecdotes Told by John Montgomery, Recalled by Jane E. Montgomery," unpublished manuscript, March 1946, SCU.

4. Jane Montgomery, "A Few Notes and Anecdotes," SCU. Named after Aeolus, the ancient Greek god of the wind, the traditional aeolian harp is essentially a wooden box containing a sounding board, with strings stretched lengthwise under tension across two bridges. Aside from being the only string instrument played solely by the wind, the aeolian harp is also the only stringed instrument that plays solely harmonic frequencies.

5. Quoted in Helen Dare, "J. J. Montgomery—The Personality of the Man," *San Francisco Call*, May 7, 1905.

6. Walker, "Oakland Rising: The Industrialization of Alameda County."

7. *AC Transit Times*, special issues of the Alameda–Contra Costa Transit District, October 1960 and September 1963. This wharf, also colloquially known as the "Oakland Mole," was later renamed the Oakland Long Wharf. This commuter service flourished for decades.

8. "Bridget Evoy," *Oakland Tribune*, March 23, 1941.

9. Baptismal Register for St. Mary's Parish, Oakland, archives of St. Patrick's Seminary, Roman Catholic Diocese of San Francisco, Menlo Park, CA, p. 128, records James P. Montgomery's baptism on March 25, 1865, sponsored by Bridget M. Evoy.

10. The moniker "Great San Francisco Earthquake" was later adopted for the much larger earthquake that occurred in the San Francisco Bay Area on April 18, 1906.

11. Family oral history as told to Marcia Jane Wendt (the author's mother) by her mother, Marie Dolores Montgomery (Ellen Evoy Montgomery's granddaughter). James Patrick Montgomery (1865–1956) was the author's great-grandfather.

12. Bridget Evoy, last will and testament, Alameda County Clerk-Recorder's Office. The will was witnessed by John McCullough and Patrick McGillian.

13. In the early 1890s the marble slab was mounted on the side of the McCourtney mausoleum within the same cemetery plot.

Chapter 11

1. Family oral history passed through Mary Ann McCourtney Belden to her daughter Blanche Belden, to Jane E. Montgomery, and then to Marcia J. Wendt, the author's mother.

2. *Sacramento Daily Union*, January 10, 1868.

3. John Evoy, "Letters of Administration in the Matter of the Estate of Bridget M. Evoy, Deceased," Alameda County Clerk-Recorder's Office. The Temescal property was valued at $973,140 in 1868.

4. Zach Montgomery, Zach, "In the matter of the Estate of B. M. Evoy, Deceased," April 6, 1868, Probate Court, Alameda County. See also Probate Case Number 210, Evoy, M. Bridget, Alameda County Probate Records, Alameda County Courthouse. Her estate was administered by John Evoy and Zach Montgomery, case commenced December 9, 1867, and closed on December 16, 1872, Probate Index Volume I for 1853–79.

5. Edward C. Prather, Map of the Evoy Tract, Oakland, Alameda County, California, 1905.

6. "Death of Mrs. Evoy," *Berkeley Daily Gazette*, November 21, 1895; "A Woman's Big Estate: Evoy had Accumulated a Fortune of $250,000," *San Francisco Examiner*, October 20, 1894.

7. The McCourtney property in Yuba County (McCourtney's Crossing) was located within Township 014N/Range 006E/Section 27 and Section 22. Margaret's property in Temescal was designated "Tract 58" on the Kellersberger map of 1852; Tract 58 was 58½ acres in size.

8. Thompson, "Early Reclamation and Abandonment." At that time, the organization of assessment districts to reclaim wetlands was transferred from the State Board of Swamp and Overflowed Land Commissioners to the auspices of county boards of supervisors.

9. Currently, Sherman Island is ten feet <u>below sea level</u> due to the drainage of wetlands in the delta, which has dried out its <u>peat soils</u>, resulting in <u>land subsidence</u>. "In . . . parts of Sherman Island, the land has now subsided 25 feet since the late 1800s—and continues to sink between half an inch and 1.5 inches yearly." Velasquez-Manoff, "Want to Prevent California's Katrina?"

10. The federal Swamp Lands Act (1850) enabled states to construct the necessary levees and drains to reclaim swampy and overflowed lands unfit for cultivation.

11. "Agricultural Notes," *Pacific Rural Press*, October 28, 1876.

12. Diane Judd, "Early Days in Temescal," unpublished thesis, Laney College, June 1980; Thompson & West, *Official and Historical Atlas of Alameda County*; Wurm, Theodore Grover, "Our Northern Suburb of Temescal," Oakland, 1991, 4.

13. Langley, *Directory of the City of Oakland.*

14. "Another Great Sale," *Daily Evening Tribune*, March 3, 1875.

15. Craig S. Harwood and Gary B. Fogel, "On the Invention of Lateral Control: Wright and Montgomery," paper presented at the American Institute of Aerospace and Astronautics Conference, AIAA SciTech Forum, January 7–11, 2019, https://www.researchgate.net/publication/330196266_On_the_Invention_of_Lateral_Control_Wright_and_Montgomery?_tp=eyJjb250ZXh0Ijp7ImZpcnN0UGFnZSI6InByb2ZpbGUiLCJwYWdlIjoicHJvZmlsZSJ9fQ. John J. Montgomery would eventually emerge as a significant American inventor and arguably the first person to achieve controlled flight in a limited fashion.

16. 1870 U.S. Population Census for Alameda County, Oakland Township.

17. Baker, *Past and Present of Alameda County.*

18. Sacred Heart Catholic Church, Oakland, California, "Get to Know Our History," https://sacredheartoak.org/get-to-know-our-history.

19. Sacred Heart Parish, *Story of Sacred Heart Church.*

20. "St. Lawrence School," *Oakland Tribune,* June 1, 1883; Elliott, *Oakland and Surroundings*; Baker, *Past and Present of Alameda County.* This school was dedicated to St. Lawrence, on June 27, 1880.

21. "St. Lawrence School," *Oakland Tribune,* June 1, 1883; Elliott, *Oakland and Surroundings*; Baker, *Past and Present of Alameda County.*

22. D. M. Bishop and Co., *Bishop's Oakland Directory*; *Who's Who in California.*

23. Merritt, *History of Alameda County.*

24. Crocker, "Who Made Oakland?" Richard Montgomery, a realtor and member of the Oakland Realty Board, was also a cofounder of the Central Oakland Improvement Club. He subdivided the former Evoy Tract (Tract No. 36) into residential lots on, 41st, 42nd, 45th, Rich, and Weber Streets.

25. Johnson, "A Temescal Pioneer."

Bibliography

Archival Collections

Office of the Alameda County Clerk, Oakland, CA (ALCC)
California State Library
    John Bidwell Papers, California State Library, Sacramento, CA (CSL)
    California Room, Sutro Library, San Francisco, CA (CSL-Sutro)
Church of Jesus Christ of Latter-Day Saints
    Microfiche collection, Family History Center, Santa Cruz, CA
    Oakland Regional Family History Center, Oakland, CA
Department of Archives and Special Collections, Fordham University, New York, NY
John J. Montgomery collection, Santa Clara University Archives and Special Collections, Santa Clara, CA (SCU)
Los Angeles Public Library, microfiche collection, California Room (LAPL)
Louis E. Stocklmeir Regional History Library and Archives, De Anza Community College, Cupertino, CA
Marysville Public Library, California Room, Marysville, CA
Nevada County Historical Society, Nevada City, CA
    Nevada County Historical Photographs
    Property owner books and historical maps
Andrew J. Russell Photograph Collection, Oakland Museum of California
Oakland Public Library Main Branch, Oakland, CA
    Newspaper microform collection
    Oakland History Center
    Temescal History Collection, compiled by Jeff Norman
Sacred Heart Parish, Oakland, CA
Property Grantee/Grantor files, Santa Clara County Archives, San Jose, CA
San Francisco Public Library, newspaper microform collection, San Francisco, CA
San José Public Library, San José, CA
    Map collection, California Room
    Newspaper microform collection
Shasta Historical Society, Redding, CA
    Book of Deeds
    Book of Mortgages
St. Patrick's Seminary, Roman Catholic Diocese of San Francisco, Menlo Park, CA

St. Louis Research Center, State Historical Society of Missouri, St. Louis, MO
Book of Deeds, Office of the County Clerk, Sutter County, Yuba City, CA
University of California–Berkeley, Berkeley, CA
    Bancroft Library (BL)
    Doe Memorial Library (newspaper microform collection)
University of California–Riverside, Riverside, CA
    Center for Bibliographical Studies and Research
    California Digital Newspaper Collection (UCR)
Yuba County Public Library, Yuba City, CA (YCPL)

Newspapers

Chico Weekly Chronicle
Daily Alta California
Daily Evening Tribune (Oakland, CA)
Marysville Daily Appeal
Marysville Daily Democrat Appeal
Marysville Daily National Democrat
Marysville Herald
The Miners Express (Dubuque, IA)
The Nevada Journal
The New York Times
Oakland Telegraph
Oakland Tribune
Pacific
Sacramento Daily Union
Sacramento Transcript
San Francisco Chronicle
San Francisco Examiner
Santa Cruz Surf
Settler's and Miner's Tribune (Sacramento, CA)
The Shasta Courier
Weekly Butte Record

Primary Sources

Allsop, Thomas, and Robert Allsop. *California and Its Gold Mines: Being a Series of Recent Communications from the Mining Districts, upon the Present Condition and Future Prospects of Quartz Mining; with an Account of the Richer Deposits, and Incidental Notices of the Climate, Scenery, and Mode of Life in California.* Groombridge and Sons, 1853.
Bates, D. B. (Mrs.). *Incidents on Land and Water: Or Four Years on the Pacific Coast.* Published by the author, 1861.
Bidwell, John. *Journal of a Trip to California in 1841.* Weston, 1844.
Britton & Co. *Official Map of Shasta County, California: Approved by the Board of Supervisors, February Term, 1862.* Library of Congress.

Bruff, Joseph Goldsborough, Georgia Willis Read, Ruth Gaines, and Frederick Webb Hodge. *Gold Rush: The Journals, Drawings, and Other Papers of J. Goldsborough Bruff, Captain, Washington City and California Mining Association, April 2, 1849–July 20, 1851.* Columbia University Press, 1949.

California Secretary of State. *California Blue Book (State Roster).* California State Printing Office, 1907.

California State Legislature. *The Statutes of California: Passed at the Fourteenth Session of the Legislature 1863: Begun on Monday the Fifth Day of January and Ended on Monday the Twenty-Seventh Day of April.* Benj. P. Avery, State Printer, 1863.

California State Legislature. *Journal of the House of the Assembly of California, at the Tenth Session of the Legislature.* O'Meara, 1859.

California Supreme Court, West Group, and Bancroft-Whitney Company. *Reports of Cases Determined in the Supreme Court of the State of California.* Bancroft-Whitney, 1887.

Clark, Thomas D. *Gold Rush Diary: Being the Journal of Elisha Douglas Perkins on the Overland Trail in the Spring and Summer of 1849.* University Press of Kentucky, 2015.

Collet, Oscar W. *Index to Instruments Affecting Real Estate Recorded in the Office of Recorder of Deeds in the County of St. Louis Mo.* Grantors, Daly & Co., Stationers, 1874.

D. M. Bishop and Co. *Bishop's Oakland Directory 1881–82.* Directory Publishing Co., 1882.

Davis, William Heath. *Sixty Years in California: A History of Events and Life in California; Personal, Political and Military, Under the Mexican Regime; During the Quasi-Military Government of the Territory by the United States, and After the Admission of the State into the Union, Being a Compilation by a Witness of the Events Described.* A. J. Leary, 1889.

Delano, Alonzo. *Across the Plains and Among the Diggings.* Wilson-Erickson, 1936.

Derby, George Horatio. "The Sacramento Valley from the American River to Butte Creek." Map drawn by order of General I. Riley, 1849.

Green, James. *Green's St. Louis Directory (No. 1) for 1845: Containing the Names of the Inhabitants, Their Occupations, Places of Business and Dwelling Houses; Also a List of the Streets and Avenues Together with Other Useful Information and an Advertisement Directory.* James Green, 1844.

Haun, Catherine Margaret. "A Woman's Trip Across the Plains in 1849." Photostat, n.d. https://d1lexza0zk46za.cloudfront.net/history/am-docs/pioneer-womans-journey.pdf.

Haynes, M. B. "Map of the County of Alameda." C. E. Thomson & West, 1878.

Heiskell, Hugh Brown, and Edward M. Steel. *A Forty-Niner from Tennessee: The Diary of Hugh Brown Heiskell.* University of Tennessee Press, 1998.

Henkenius, J. C. "Map of the City of Oakland and Surroundings: Compiled from Official and Private Surveys." Woodward and Gamble, 1888.

Keemle, Charles. *The St. Louis Directory for the Years 1840–1.* Riverside Press, 1840.

Keim, De B. Randolph. *Society in Washington: Its Noted Men, Accomplished Women, Established Customs, and Notable Events.* Harrisburg, 1887.

Kellersberger, Julius G. "Map of the Ranchos of Vicente & Domingo Peralta Containing 16,970.68 Acres, Oakland, California," 1852.

King, M. G., and William J. Dingee. "Map of Oakland, Berkeley and Alameda." Taggart & Dingee, 1878.

Langley, H. G. *A Directory of the City of Oakland and Its Environs, Including Alameda, Berkeley, and Temescal.* Strickland & Co. and H. G. Langley, 1874.

"Message from the President of the United States, in Answer to a Resolution of the Senate, Calling for Further Information in Relation to the Formation of a State Government in California; and Also, in Relation to the Condition of Civil Affairs in Oregon. Read May 22, 1850. Ordered to Be Printed, May 29." S. Ex. Doc. 31-52, 31st Cong., 1st Sess., May 22, 1850. https://www.govinfo.gov/app/details/SERIALSET-00561_00_00-006-0052-0000.

Miller, Joaquin. *Joaquin Miller's Romantic Life Amongst the Red Indians: An Autobiography.* Saxon, 1890.

Phelps, Alonzo, John Muir, John LeConte, and Caleb T. Fay. *Contemporary Biography of California's Representative Men, with Contributions from Distinguished Scholars and Scientists,* A. L. Bancroft, 1882.

Reeve, Clayton, and Rebecca Foster Reeve. "From Tennessee to California in 1849: Letters of the Reeve Family of Medford New Jersey," edited by Oscar Winther. *Journal of the Rutgers University Library* 11, no. 2 (1943): 33–84.

Riley, Bennet. "The Sacramento Valley from the American River to Butte Creek." Map. Government Printing Office, 1849.

Stilwell, B. F. *Directory of the Township and City of Oakland: Together with the Townships of Brooklyn and Alameda, for the Year 1869.* Oakland News Office, 1869.

US Army Corps of Topographical Engineers. *An Expedition to the Valley of the Great Salt Lake of Utah: Including a Description of Its Geography, Natural History, and Minerals, and an Analysis of Its Waters; with an Authentic Account of the Mormon Settlement . . . Also, a Reconnaissance of a New Route Through the Rocky Mountains. And Two Large and Accurate Maps of That Region.* Lippincott, Grambo, 1855.

United States Coast Survey, J. Alden, A. Blondeau, R. D. Cutts, W. M. C. Fairfax, J. Knight, J. Lambert, G. Mathiot, G. B. Metzeroth, W. R. Palmer, J. J. Ricketts, and A. F. Rodgers. *Entrance to San Francisco Bay California.* US Coast Survey Office, 1859.

Secondary Sources

Adams, E. Francis. *Oakland's Early History.* City Council of Oakland, 1932.

Akins, Damon, B., and William J. Hurtado. *We Are the Land: A History of Native California.* University of California Press, 2021.

Alexander, Thomas G. *Brigham Young and the Expansion of the Mormon Faith.* University of Oklahoma Press, 2019.

Almquist, E. L. "Pre-Famine Ireland and the Theory of European Proto-Industrialization: Evidence from the 1841 Census." *Journal of Economic History* 39 (1979): 699–718.

Alpers, Charles N., Michael P. Hunerlach, Jason T. May, and Roger L. Hothem. "Mercury Contamination from Historic Gold Mining in California." Version 1.1. US Geological Survey, November 2005. https://pubs.usgs.gov/fs/2005/3014/.

Alvarez, Dick. "Emigrant Camp Investigation." Passport in Time. Lassen National Forest, California, 2000. https://octa-trails.org/wp-content/uploads/2023/06/2000-Emigrant-Camp-2000-Passport-in-Time.pdf?srsltid=AfmBOop TkpdNYtIOMrJhAid14lXDc-1x6D-bod8sM-d0jxr7Tv6Di-wc.

Ambro, Richard D. "The Spanish Colonial Era in Emeryville and the East Bay (1772–1848)." In *Early Emeryville Remembered: Historical Essays & Photographs*. Emeryville Historical Society, 1996.

Anderson Kat. *Tending the Wild: Native American Knowledge and the Management of California's Natural Resources*. University of California Press, 2005.

Angulo, Jaime de. *Indians in Overalls*. City Lights Books. 1990.

Armitage, Susan, H., and Elizabeth Jameson. *The Women's West*. University of Oklahoma Press, 1987.

Arrigoni, Aimee, "The First Decades of a New Era: The Native Americans of the East Bay After the Gold Rush." Museum of the San Ramon Valley, 2003. https://museumsrv.org/the-first-decades-of-a-new-era-the-native-americans-of-the-east-bay-after-the-gold-rush/.

Bagley, Will. *Across the Plains, Mountains, and Deserts: A Bibliography of the Oregon-California Trail, 1812–1912*. Prairie Dog Press, 2014.

Bagley, Will. *With Golden Visions Bright Before Them: Trails to the Mining West, 1849–1852*. University of Oklahoma Press, 2012.

Baker, Joseph E. *Past and Present of Alameda County, California*. S. J. Clarke, 1914.

Ballou, Mary B. *"I Hear the Hogs in My Kitchen": A Woman's View of the Gold Rush*. Printed for F. W. Beinecke, 1962.

Bancroft, Hubert Howe. *California Inter Pocula*. San Francisco: History Co., 1888.

Bancroft, Hubert Howe. *History of California*. 7 vols. San Francisco: History Co., 1884–90.

Bancroft, Hubert Howe. *History of the Pacific States of North America*. 34 vols. San Francisco: A. L. Bancroft, 1882–90.

Bean, Edwin F. *Bean's History and Directory of Nevada County, California*. Daily Gazette Books, 1867.

Beebe, Rose Marie, and Robert M. Senkewicz. *Testimonios: Early California Through the Eyes of Women, 1815–1848*. University of Oklahoma Press, 2015.

Bidwell, John, Michael J. Gillis, and Michael F Magliari. *John Bidwell and California: The Life and Writings of a Pioneer, 1841–1900*. A. H. Clark, 2004.

Bidwell, John, Milo Milton Quaife, and John Steele. *Echoes of the Past About California*. Kessinger, n.d.

Boggs, Mae Hélène Bacon. *My Playhouse Was a Concord Coach: An Anthology of Newspaper Clippings and Documents Relating to Those Who Made California History During the Years 1822–1888; Compiled by Mae Hélène Bacon*. Printed at the Howell-North Press, 1942.

Bowie, Augustus Jesse. *A Practical Treatise on Hydraulic Mining in California: With Description of the Use and Construction of Ditches, Flumes, Wrought-Iron Pipes, and Dams*. D. Van Nostrand, 1885.

Bowman, J. N. "The Birthdays of Urban Communities (Oakland and Berkeley)." *California Historical Society Quarterly* 31 (1922): 333.

Bowman J. N. "The Peraltas and Their Houses." *California Historical Society Quarterly* 30, no. 3 (1951): 217–31.

Bozich, Frank A. "The Unwanted Immigrant." Honors Program Project, Department of History, James Madison University, 2016. https://commons.lib.jmu.edu/cgi/viewcontent.cgi?article=1194&context=honors201019.

Breen Richard. "Dowry Payments and the Irish Case." *Comparative Studies in Society and History* 26, no. 2 (1984): 280–96.

Brennan, Paul. "The Family in Ireland." *Etudes Irlandaises* 29, no. 1 (2004): 95–102.

Brown G. Chester, and the California State Mining Bureau. *Mines and Mineral Resources of Shasta County, Siskiyou County, Trinity County*, State Printing Office, 1915.

Buck, D. E., and D. Moorman. *A Guide to the Lassen Trail and Burnett Cutoff.* Emigrant Trails West Series Guidebook. Trails West, 2015.

Burich, Keith R. "Philip T. Tyson: The Jeremiah of the Gold Rush." *Southern California Quarterly* 79, no. 4 (1997): 409–30.

Burrill, Richard, Tehama County Museum, and California State University–Chico. *Historical and Archaeological Investigations of the Hi Good Cabin Site Ca-Teh-2105h: Tehama County California.* Anthro, 2010.

Chamberlain, William H. *History of Sutter County, California.* Thompson & West, 1879.

Chamberlain, William H., and Harry Laurenz Wells. *History of Yuba County, California, with Illustrations Descriptive of Its Scenery, Residences, Public Buildings, Fine Blocks, and Manufactories.* Thompson & West, 1879.

Chandler, Robert J. "California's 1863 Loyalty Oaths: Another Look." *Arizona and the West* 21, no. 3 (1979): 215–34.

City of Berkeley. "Cultural Resources Technical Report." Appendix C in *Adeline Corridor Specific Plan, Draft Environmental Impact Report.* Department of Planning and Development, City of Berkeley, 2018.

Clark, Carole Ann. "Crow and Cheyenne Women: Some Differences in Their Roles as Related to Tribal History." Graduate thesis. University of Montana, 1969.

Clay, Karen B. "Property Rights and Institutions: Congress and the California Land Act of 1851." *Journal of Economic History* 59, no. 1 (1999): 122–42.

Clemmer, Richard, O. "The Tail of the Elephant: Indians in Emigrant Diaries, 1842–1862." *Nevada Historical Society Quarterly* 30, no. 4 (1987): 269–90.

Cogan, Frances B. *All-American Girl: The Ideal of Real Womanhood in Mid-Nineteenth-Century America.* University of Georgia Press, 2010.

Colville, Samuel. *Colville's Marysville Directory for the Year Commencing November 1, 1855: Embracing a General Directory of Citizens, an Appendix of General Information, Etc., Together with a Historical Sketch of Marysville.* Research Publications, 1961.

Comstock, David A. *News & Advertising in the Early Gold Camps of Nevada County, California (1850–1874).* Bonanza Press, 2019.

Conway, Thomas G. "The Extension of the Poor Law to Ireland." PhD diss., Loyola University of Chicago, 1969.

Cott, Nancy F., and Elizabeth H. Pleck. *A Heritage of Her Own: Toward a New Social History of American Women*. ACLS History E-Book Project, 2008.

Creely, Elizabeth. "Irish 1851: Historical Essay." Found SF, the San Francisco Digital History Archive. 2002. https://www.foundsf.org/index.php?title=Irish_1851.

Crocker, Florence B. "Who Made Oakland?" C. Dalton, 1925.

Cruea, Susan M. "Changing Ideals of Womanhood During the Nineteenth-Century Woman Movement." *University Writing Program Faculty Publications* 1 (2005). https://scholarworks.bgsu.edu/gsw_pub/1.

Culmer, Frederic Arthur. "'General' John Wilson, Signer of the Deseret Petition Including Letters from the Leonard Collection." *California Historical Society Quarterly* 26 (1947): 321–48.

Davis, Winfield J. *History of Political Conventions in California 1849–1892*. California State Library, 1893.

Davis, Winfield J. *An Illustrated History of Sacramento County, California*. Lewis, 1890.

Delay, Peter J. *History of Yuba and Sutter Counties, California*, Historic Record Co., 1924.

Delano, Alonzo, and Irving McKee. *Alonzo Delano's California Correspondence: Being Letters Hitherto Uncollected from the "Ottawa (Illinois) Free Trader" and the "New Orleans True Delta," 1849–1952*. Sacramento Book Collectors Club, 1952.

Denig, Edwin Thompson, and John C Ewers. *Five Indian Tribes of the Upper Missouri: Sioux, Arickaras, Assiniboines, Crees, Crows*. University of Oklahoma Press, 1977.

Derby, George Horatio. *The Army Surveys of Gold Rush California: Reports of the Topographical Engineers, 1849–1851* Arthur H. Clark, 2015.

Deverell, William, and Anne Farrar Hyde. *A History of North America to 1877*. Vol. 1 of *Shaped by the West*. University of California Press, 2018.

Dixon, Kelly L. "The Donner Party: An Archaeological Perspective on a Tragedy in the Sierras." *Historical Methods* 40, no. 4 (2007): 179–80.

Durham, David L. *California's Geographic Names: A Gazetteer of Historic and Modern Names of the State*. Word Dancer Press, 1998.

Durham, Walter T. *Volunteer Forty-Niners: Tennesseans and the California Gold Rush*. Vanderbilt University Press, 1997.

Elliott W. W. *Oakland and Surroundings*. W. W. Elliott, 1885.

Emmons, Ann, and Theodore Catton. *Lassen Volcanic National Park Historic Resources Study*. Report prepared for the National Park Service. Historical Research Associates, 2003.

Engineering and Mining Journal 86, no. 4 (July 25, 1908): 181.

Enzler, Jerry A. *Jim Bridger: Trailblazer of the American West*. University of Oklahoma Press, 2021.

Faye, Paul-Louis. "Notes on the Southern Maidu." *University of California Publications in American Archaeology and Ethnology* 20, no. 3 (1923): 35–53.

Field, Stephen J. *Personal Reminiscences of Early Days in California: With Other Sketches*. No publisher, 1880.

Frank B. F., and H. W Chappell. *The History and Business Directory of Shasta County: Comprising an Accurate Historical Sketch of the County from Its Earliest Settlement to the Present Time*. Redding Independent Book and Job Printing House, 1881.

Furlong, Nicholas. *The Mighty Wave: The 1798 Rebellion in Wexford, Ireland.* Four Courts Press, 1996.

Giles, Rosena A. *Shasta County, California: A History.* Foreword by Joseph A. Sullivan. Biobooks, 1949.

Gordon, Christopher Alan. *Fire, Pestilence, and Death: St. Louis, 1849.* Missouri Historical Society Press, 2018.

Gudde, Erwin Gustav. *California Gold Camps: A Geographical and Historical Dictionary of Camps, Towns, and Localities Where Gold Was Found and Mined; Wayside Stations and Trading Centers.* University of California Press, 1975.

Gudde, Erwin Gustav, and Elisabeth K. Gudde. *California Gold Camps: A Geographical and Historical Dictionary of Camps, Towns, and Localities Where Gold Was Found and Mined; Wayside Stations and Trading Centers.* Berkeley: University of California Press, 2009.

Gudde, Erwin Gustav. *California Place Names: The Origin and Etymology of Current Geographical Names,* edited by William Bright. 4th ed. University of California Press, 2010. https://doi.org/10.1525/9780520355026.

Guinn, J. M. *History of the State of California and Biographical Record of Oakland and Environs, Also Containing Biographies of Well-Known Citizens of the Past and Present.* Vol. 2. Historic Record Co., 1907.

Guinn, J. M. *History of the State of California and Biographical Record of the Sacramento Valley, California: An Historical Story of the State's Marvelous Growth from Its Earliest Settlement to the Present Time.* Chapman, 1906.

Hafen, LeRoy R., and Ann W. Hafen, eds. *Fremont's Fourth Expedition: A Documentary Account of the Disaster of 1848–1849, with Diaries, Letters, and Reports by Participants in the Tragedy.* Arthur H. Clark, 1960.

Hague, Harlan, and David J. Langum. *Thomas O. Larkin: A Life of Patriotism and Profit in Old California.* University of Oklahoma Press, 1990.

Halley, William. *The Centennial Year Book of Alameda County, California: Containing a Summary of the Discovery and Settlement of California, a Description of the Contra Costa Under Spanish Mexican and American Rule, an Account of the Organization and Settlement of Alameda County . . . Also a Gazetteer of Each Township, Useful Local and General Statistical Information Appropriate for the Present Time to Which Are Added Biographical Sketches of Prominent Pioneers and Public Men.* W. Halley, 1876.

Hardesty, D. L. "The Archaeology of the Donner Party Tragedy." *Nevada Historical Society Quarterly* 30, no. 4 (1987): 246–58. https://epubs.nsla.nv.gov/statepubs/epubs/210777-1987-4Winter.pdf.

Harper, Bethany S. "The Influence of Jane Austen's Works on Societal Attitudes Regarding Women and Marriage, Education. and Slavery from the Early Nineteenth Century." Bachelor's thesis, Department of History and Department of English, California State University–Stanislaus, 2020.

Harwood, Craig S., and Gary B. Fogel. *Quest for Flight: John J. Montgomery and the Dawn of Aviation in the West.* University of Oklahoma Press, 2012.

Haynes, Bessie Doak, and Edgar Haynes. *The Grizzly Bear; Portraits from Life.* University of Oklahoma Press, 1966.

Heizer, Robert F., ed. *They Were Only Diggers: A Collection of Articles from California Newspapers, 1851–1866, on Indian and White Relations.* Ballena Press, 1974.

Helfrich, Devere, and Helen Helfrich. "The Applegate Trail." *Journal of the Shaw Historical Library* 10 (1996).

Herringshaw, Thomas. *Herringshaw's Encyclopedia of American Biography of the Nineteenth Century. Accurate and Succinct Biographies of Famous Men and Women in All Walks of Life Who Are or Have Been the Acknowledged Leaders of Life and Thought of the United States Since Its Formation.* American Publishers Association, 1898.

Hinkel, Edgar Joseph, and William E. McCann. *Oakland 1852–1938: Some Phases of the Social, Political, and Economic History of Oakland, California, 1852–1938.* Oakland Free Library and US Works Progress Administration, 1939.

Holliday, J. S. "In the Diggings." *California History* 61, no. 3 (1982): 168–87.

Holliday, J. S., and William Swain, *The World Rushed In: The California Gold Rush Experience.* University of Oklahoma Press, 2002.

Howell, Elijah Preston, Susan Badger Doyle, and Donald E. Buck. *The 1849 California Trail Diaries of Elijah Preston Howell.* Oregon-California Trails Association, 1995.

Hughes, Edan Milton. *Artists in California, 1786–1940.* 2nd ed. Hughes, 1989.

Hurley, Mark J. *Church-State Relations in Education in California.* Catholic University of America, 1948.

Hurtado, Albert L. *Indian Survival on the California Frontier.* Yale University Press, 1998.

Hurtado, Albert L. "Indians in Town and Country: The Nisenan Indians' Changing Economy and Society as Shown in John A. Sutter's 1856 Correspondence." *American Indian Culture and Research Journal* 12, no. 2 (1988).

Hyman, Harold M. "New Light on *Cohen v. Wright*: California's First Loyalty Oath Case." *Pacific Historical Review* 28 (1959): 131–40.

Isenberg Andrew C. *The California Gold Rush: A Brief History with Documents.* Bedford/St. Martin's, 2018.

Isenberg Andrew C. *Mining California: An Ecological History.* Hill and Wang, 2005.

Johnson, Hal. "So We're Told." *Berkeley Daily Gazette,* December 19, 20, 24, and 26, 1951.

Johnson, Hal, "A Temescal Pioneer," *Berkeley Daily Gazette,* December 19, 1951.

Judd, Diane, R. "Early Days in Temescal," *Oakland Heritage Alliance Newsletter* 4, no. 1 (1984): 1–6.

Khan, B. Zorina. "Married Women's Property Laws and Female Commercial Activity: Evidence from United States Patent Records, 1790–1895." *Journal of Economic History* 56, no. 2 (1996): 356–88.

Krahe, D., and Theodore Catton. "Little Gem of the Cascades: An Administrative History of Lassen Volcanic National Park. University of Montana, 2010. https://npshistory.com/publications/lavo/adhi.pdf.

Kraus, Michael. "Across the Western Sea (1783–1845)." *Journal of British Studies* 1, no. 2 (1962): 91–114.

Kroeber, Theodora. *Ishi in Two Worlds: A Biography of the Last Wild Indian in North America.* University of California Press, 1965.

Kurtz, Patricia Lindgren. *Mountain Maidu and Pioneers: A History of Indian Valley, Plumas County, California, 1850–1920.* iUniverse, 2010.

Lass William E. *Navigating the Missouri: Steamboating on Nature's Highway, 1819–1935.* Arthur H. Clark, 2008.

Layton, Thomas N. "From Pottage to Portage: A Perspective on Aboriginal Horse Use in the Northern Great Basin Prior to 1850." *Nevada Historical Society Quarterly* 20, no. 4 (1978): 241–51.

Layton, Thomas N. "Stalking Elephants in Nevada." *Western Folklore* 35, no. 4 (1976): 250–57.

Leek, Nancy. *John Bidwell: The Adventurous Life of a California Pioneer.* Association for Northern California Historical Research, 2010.

Lerner, Gerda. *The Lady and the Mill Girl: Changes in the Status of Women in the Age of Jackson.* Warner Modular, 1973.

Levy, JoAnn. *They Saw the Elephant: Women in the California Gold Rush.* University of Oklahoma Press, 1992.

Lewis, Graham M. "Regional Ideas and Reality in the Cis–Rocky Mountain West." *Transactions of the Institute of British Geographers* 38 (1966): 135–50.

Lewis Publishing Co. *A Memorial and Biographical History of Northern California.* Lewis Publishing, 1891.

Lightfoot, Kent G., Otis Parrish Lee, M. Panich Tsim, D. Schneider, and K. Elizabeth Soluri. *California Indians and Their Environment: An Introduction.* University of California Press, 2009.

Madden, Richard. *The United Irishmen: Their Lives and Times.* J. Madden & Co., 1843.

Madley, Benjamin. *An American Genocide: The United States and the California Indian Catastrophe, 1846–1873.* Yale University Press, 2017.

Mann, Ralph. *After the Gold Rush: Society in Grass Valley and Nevada City, California, 1849–1870.* Stanford University Press, 1982.

Marshall, Willis Woodbury. "Geography of the Early Port of St. Louis." PhD diss, Washington University, 1932.

Maxwell, Ian. *Everyday Life in Nineteenth-Century Ireland: Poverty, Politics, and the Irish People.* History Press, 2011.

McCabe, Ciarán. *Begging, Charity, and Religion in Pre-Famine Ireland.* Liverpool University Press, 2018.

McCullagh, Ciaran. "A Tie That Blinds: Family and Ideology in Ireland." *Economic and Social Review* 22, no. 3, (1991): 199–211.

Merritt, Frank Clinton. *History of Alameda County, California.* S. J. Clarke, 1928.

Mikesell, Stephen. "The Suspension Bridges of Andrew Smith Hallidie." *California History* 95, no. 2 (2018): 52–70.

Milliken, Randall. *A Time of Little Choice: The Disintegration of Tribal Culture in the San Francisco Bay Area, 1769–1810.* Ballena Press, 1995.

Milliken, Randall, Laurence H. Shoup, and Beverly R. Ortiz. *Ohlone/Costanoan Indians of the San Francisco Peninsula and Their Neighbors, Yesterday and Today.* Archaeological and Historical Consultants, 2009.

Montgomery, Zach. *The Poison Fountain, or Anti-Parental Education: Essays and Discussions on the School Question from a Parental and Non-Sectarian Standpoint.* Z. Montgomery, 1878.

National Park Service. "Women Traveling West." The Emigrant Experience. https://www.nps.gov/articles/000/women-traveling-west.htm.

Nicholas, Stephen, and Richard H. Steckel. "Tall but Poor: Living Standards of Men and Women in Pre-Famine Ireland." *Journal of European Economic History* 26, no. 1 (1997): 105.

Norman, Jeff, *Temescal Legacies: Narratives of Change from a North Oakland Neighborhood*. Shared Ground, 2006.

Noy, Gary. *Gold Rush Stories: 49 Tales of Seekers, Scoundrels, Loss, and Luck*. Sierra College Press, 2017.

"Oakland and Her Improvements." *California Farmer and Journal of Useful Sciences* 21, no. 21 (1864).

O'Hara, Patricia. *Partners in Production? Women, Farm, and Family in Ireland*. Berghahn Books, 1998.

Olmsted, David L., and Omer C. Stewart. "Achumawi." In *Handbook of North American Indians*. Vol. 8, *California*, edited by Robert F. Heizer, 225–35. Smithsonian Institution, 1978.

Osborne, Andrew Jackson. *J. Granville Doll and the Formative Years of Red Bluff*. Association for Northern California Records and Research, 1985.

Peden, Joseph R. *Opposition to Public Education in California: Zach Montgomery's Alternative Model for the Public School System of California, 1861–1885*. Pacific Coast History of Education Society, 1979.

Purdy, Harry L. *An Historical Analysis of the Economic Growth of St. Louis 1945*. Federal Reserve Archival System, 1945.

Raftery, Deirdre, and Catriona Delaney. "Irish Nuns and Education in the Anglophone World, 1800–1900." *Feminist Theology* 30, no. 3 (2022): 245–61.

Ramey, Earl. "The Beginnings of Marysville: Part I." *California Historical Society Quarterly* 14, no. 3 (1935): 195–229.

Ramey, Earl, "The Beginnings of Marysville: Part II." *California Historical Society Quarterly* 14, no. 4 (1935): 375–407.

Ramey, Earl, "The Cheever Family and the Founding of Yuba City." *Bulletin of the Sutter County Historical Society* 2, no. 7 (1960): 2–9.

Ramey, Earl. "Edward Cheever and the Founding of Yuba City." *Bulletin of the Sutter County Historical Society* 48, no. 7 (2004): 12–20.

Ramey, Earl. "The Election of 1860 in Sutter and Yuba Counties." *Bulletin of the Sutter County Historical Society* 3, no. 1 (1962): 1–20.

Ramey, Earl. "Yuba City's Birthday." *Bulletin of the Sutter County Historical Society* 9, no. 2 (1970): 2–14.

Rawls, James J. *Indians of California: The Changing Image*. University of Oklahoma Press, 1984.

Read, Georgia Willis. "Diseases, Drugs and Doctors on the Oregon-California Trail in the Gold-Rush Years." *Missouri Historical Review* 38, no. 3 (1944): 260–76.

Read, Georgia Willis. "Women and Children on the Oregon-California Trail in the Gold-Rush Years." *Missouri Historical Review* 38, no. 1 (1944): 1–23.

Reid, Bernard, J., and Mary McDougall Gordon. *Overland to California with the Pioneer Line: The Gold Rush Diary of Bernard J. Reid*. University of Illinois Press, 1987.

Rogers, Fred Blackburn. *Bear Flag Lieutenant: The Life Story of Henry L. Ford, 1822–1860*. California Historical Society, 1951.

Royce, Sarah. *A Frontier Lady: Recollections of the Gold Rush and Early California*. University of Nebraska Press, 1977.

Sacred Heart Parish, Oakland. *The Story of Sacred Heart Church, Oakland California; and the Bicentennial History of Catholic America*. Limited ed. Custombook, 1976.

Sapir, Edward, and Leslie Spier. *Notes on the Culture of the Yana*. Coyote Press, 1943.

Savage, Mary Lucida. *The Congregation of Saint Joseph of Carondelet: A Brief Account of Its Origin and Its Work in the United States (1650–1922)*. B. Herder, 1927.

Sayenga, Donald. "Contextual Essay on Wire Bridges: John A. Roeblings' Sons Co., Trenton, Mercer County, New Jersey." *Historic American Engineering Record* (1999).

Scannell, Daniel. *The Story of St. Theresa Parish*. St. Theresa Parish, 2001.

Scott, Franklin D. "Peter Lassen: Danish Pioneer of California." *Southern California Quarterly* 63, no. 2 (1981): 113–36.

Shanahan, John Joseph. "Zachariah Montgomery: Agitator for State and Individual Rights." Master's thesis, University of California–Berkeley, 1955.

Shepherd, Frances. "Yuba Co. Development from Thompson & West History of Yuba Co." *Digger's Digest* (Sutter–Yuba County Genealogical Society) 3, no. 3 (1976): 157.

Shasta County Historical Society. *Covered Wagon*. Shasta County Historical Society, 1991.

Shuck, Oscar T. *History of the Bench and Bar of California*. Commercial Printing House, 1901.

Smith, Dottie. *The Dictionary of Early Shasta County History*. 2nd ed. Dottie Smith, 1999.

Smith, Dottie. *Ordinary Women with Extraordinary Stories from Shasta, Tehama, & Trinity Counties*. Shasta College Museum and Research Center, 2001.

Smith-Rosenberg, Carroll. *Disorderly Conduct: Visions of Gender in Victorian America*. Oxford University Press, 1985.

Solberg, Winton U. "The Sabbath on the Overland Trail to California." *Church History* 59, no. 3 (1990): 340–55.

Spearman, Arthur D. *John J. Montgomery: Father of Basic Flying*. Santa Clara University, 1967.

Stagnero, Raymond V. "Kentuckian Views Gold-Mad Sacramento (Zachariah Montgomery)." *Academy Scrapbook* (Academy Guild Press for the Academy of California Church History) 5 (1959): 232–48.

Steger, Gertrude A., and Helen Hinckley Jones. *Place Names of Shasta County*. Rev. ed. La Siesta Press, 1966.

Sweeney, John David. *The Lassen Trail: Its Course, Its Hardships, Its Heroes; an Address*. Gerber Star, 1930.

Thompson, John. "Early Reclamation and Abandonment of the Central Sacramento–San Joaquin Delta." *Sacramento History Journal* 6, no. 1–4 (2006).

Thompson & West. *Official and Historical Atlas of Alameda County, California.* Oakland: Thompson & West, 1878.

Tinkham, George H. *California and the Civil War, Extracted from Panama-Pacific Exposition Edition (1915) of California Men and Events, 1769–1890,* 1915.

Twain, Mark. *Roughing It.* Oxford University Press, 1996.

Tweet, Roald D., and National Waterways Study. *History of Transportation on the Upper Mississippi & Illinois Rivers.* National Waterways Study, US Army Engineer Water Resources Support Center, Institute for Water Resources, 1983.

Tyson Philip Thomas, George Horatio Derby, Edward Otho, Cresap Ord, Persifor Frazer Smith, Theodore Talbot, R. S. Williamson, and Bennett Riley. *Geology and Industrial Resources of California.* Wm. Minifie, 1851.

Tyson, Philip Thomas, Persifor Frazer Smith, Bennett Riley, Theodore Talbot, Edward Otho, Cresap Ord, John Fries Frazer, George Horatio Derby, and R. S Williamson. *Report of the Secretary of War Communicating Information in Relation to the Geology and Topography of California.* Government Printing Office, 1850.

Unruh, John David. *The Plains Across: The Overland Emigrants and the Trans-Mississippi West, 1840–60.* University of Illinois Press, 1979.

US Geological Survey. *Tertiary Gold-Bearing Channel Gravel in Northern Nevada County California.* Government Printing Office, 1968.

US National Park Service. *National Historic Trails: Auto Tour Route Interpretive Guide: The Tangle of Trails Through Idaho.* National Park Service, National Trails System Branch, 2008. https://www.nps.gov/orgs/1453/upload/National -Historic-Trails-Auto-Tour-Route-Interpretive-Guide-Across-Idaho.pdf.

Utley, Robert M. *A Life Wild and Perilous: Mountain Men and the Paths to the Pacific.* Henry Holt, 1998.

Van Ee, P. "Women on the Move: Overland Journeys to California." Legends of America, 2001. https://www.legendsofamerica.com/we-womenmove/.

Vaughan, Trudy, Eric W. Ritter, and Dottie Smith. *Gold and Lumber: Two Papers on Northern California History and Archaeology.* US Bureau of Land Management, 1992.

Velasquez-Manoff, Moises. "Want to Prevent California's Katrina? Grow a Marsh." *Bay Nature,* September 16, 2019.

Verbarg, Leonard H. *Celebrities at Your Doorstep.* Alameda County Historical Society, 1972.

Wagner, Theodore, George Sandow, and Britton & Rey. "Map Showing Portions of Alameda and Contra Costa Counties, City and County of San Francisco, California, Carefully Compiled from Official and Private Maps, Surveys, and Data. San Francisco: Britton & Rey, 1894. https://www.loc.gov/item/2012590175/.

Walker, Richard, "Oakland Rising: The Industrialization of Alameda County." In *The Manufactured Metropolis,* edited by Robert Lewis. Temple University Press, 2005.

Walsh, Margaret. "Women's Place on the American Frontier." *Journal of American Studies* 29, no. 2 (1995): 241–55.

Ware, Joseph E. *The Emigrants' Guide to California.* Ye Galleon Press, 1999.

Wayman, Norbury L., and St. Louis City Planning Commission. *History: Physical Growth of the City of St. Louis.* St. Louis City Planning Commission, 1969.

Webb, Benedict Joseph. *The Centenary of Catholicity in Kentucky.* C. A. Rogers, 1884.

Weber, Francis J. *Catholic Footprints in California.* Hogarth Press, 1970.

Weber, Francis J. *Encyclopedia of California's Catholic Heritage, 1769–1999.* St. Francis Historical Society and Arthur H. Clark, 2001.

Weber, Francis J. *Readings in California Catholic History.* Westernlore Press, 1967.

Wells, Harry Laurenz, Frank T. Gilbert, and W. L. Chambers. *History of Butte County, California.* H. L. Wells, 1882.

Welter, Barbara. *Dimity Convictions: The American Woman in the Nineteenth Century.* Ohio University Press, 1976.

Wheat, Carl I. "California's Bantam Cock: The Journals of Charles E. DeLong, 1858 through 1861." *California Historical Society Quarterly* 31 (1930): 245–381; 32 (1931): 165–282; 43 (1941): 20; 46 (1967): 154.

Whitney Josiah D. *The Auriferous Gravels of the Sierra Nevada of California.* Cambridge University Press, 1880.

Whitney Josiah D. *Lecture on Geology: Delivered Before the Legislature of California at San Francisco, Thursday Evening, Feb. 27 1862.* Benj. P. Avery, state printer, 1862.

Wheatland Historical Society. *Wheatland.* Arcadia, 2009.

Who's Who in California; a Biographical Directory; Being a History of California. Who's Who Publishing, 1928.

Wilde, Jane Francesca Elgee. *Ancient Legends, Mystic Charms, and Superstitions of Ireland with Sketches of the Irish Past. To Which Is Appended a Chapter on "The Ancient Race of Ireland."* Ticknor and Co., 1888.

Wilkerson, Gregg, and David Lawler. *Roadside Geology and Mining History of the Mother Lode.* Bakersfield District Office, Bureau of Land Management, 1994.

Wilson, Linda. "Constrained by Zeal: Women in Mid-Nineteenth-Century Nonconformist Churches." *Journal of Religious History* 23, no. 2 (1999): 185–202.

Wilson, Luzena Stanley, and Correnah Wilson Wright. *Luzena Stanley Wilson, '49er: Memories Recalled Years Later for Her Daughter Correnah Wilson Wright.* Eucalyptus Press, 1937.

Wollenberg, Charles. *Berkeley: A City in History.* University of California Press, 2008.

Woodham-Smith, Cecil. *The Great Hunger: Ireland, 1845–1849.* Penguin, 1962.

Index

References to illustrations are in italics.

www.ingramcontent.com/pod-product-compliance
Lightning Source LLC
Chambersburg PA
CBHW020347100426
42812CB00035B/3389/J